WRITING ABOUT

THE

HUMANITIES

WRITING ABOUT
THE
HUMANITIES

ROBERT DiYANNI

PRENTICE HALL, Upper Saddle River, New Jersey 07458

Library of Congress Cataloging-in-Publication Data

DiYanni, Robert.
    Writing about the humanities / Robert DiYanni.
        p.   cm.
    Includes index.
    ISBN 0-13-022994-6
    1. English language—Rhetoric.   2. Humanities—Research—
Methodology.   3. Humanities—Authorship.   4. Criticism—Authorship.
5. Academic writing.   I. Title.
PE1408.D593   2000
808'.042—dc21   99-31940
                                                              CIP

Editor-in-Chief: Charlyce Jones-Owen
Publisher: Bud Therien
Managing Editor: Jan Stephan
Production Liaison: Fran Russello
Editorial / Production Supervision:
    Joseph Barron / P. M. Gordon Associates, Inc.
Prepress and Manufacturing Buyer:
    Lynn Pearlman
Art Director: Jayne Conte

Cover Designer: Joe Sengotta
Director, Image Resource Center: Melinda Lee Reo
Manager, Rights and Permissions: Kay Dellosa
Image Specialist: Beth Boyd
Photo Researcher: Abby Reip
Marketing Manager: Sheryl Adams
Copy Editor: Sue Gleason
Permissions Editor: Beth Mullen

This book was set in 11/13 Times Roman by BookMasters, Inc.
and was printed and bound by Courier Companies, Inc.
The cover was printed by Phoenix Color Corp.

Acknowledgments appear on page 156,
which constitutes a continuation of the copyright page.

Printed in the United States of America

10   9   8   7   6   5   4   3   2   1

ISBN 0-13-022994-6

Prentice-Hall International (UK) Limited, *London*
Prentice-Hall of Australia Pty. Limited, *Sydney*
Prentice-Hall of Canada Inc., *Toronto*
Prentice-Hall Hispanoamericana, S.A., *Mexico*
Prentice-Hall of India Private Limited, *New Delhi*
Prentice-Hall of Japan, Inc., *Tokyo*
Person Education Asia Pte. Ltd., *Singapore*
Editora Prentice-Hall do Brasil, Ltda., *Rio de Janeiro*

For Bud Therien and Phil Miller

CONTENTS

3   Writing a Comparison   38

4   Writing from Different Critical Perspectives   51

5   Writing About Art and Music   64

6   Writing About Literature   82

7   Writing with Sources   108

PREFACE

Writing About the Humanities is designed for students in introductory humanities courses, but it can be used by students in introductory literature and art history courses as well. The first half of the book—Chapters 1 through 4—covers general issues in writing about the humanities disciplines, including how to respond to, interpret, and evaluate different types of artworks. The second half of the book—Chapters 5 through 8—focuses more specifically on writing in literature and the arts, as well as on the particulars of writing with and documenting sources. An appendix on writing essay examinations concludes the book.

Among the book's distinctive and practical features are the following:

- Consideration of multiple approaches to artworks, including responding, interpreting, and evaluating
- An approach to interpretation that includes the steps of observing, connecting, inferring, and concluding.
- A set of guidelines that summarize the key features of the writing process: drafting, organizing, revising, editing, proofreading, and comparing
- Writing exercises and assignments
- Sample student papers in various disciplines
- Examples of professional writing in different disciplines
- Critical perspectives exemplified
- Guidance in researching and writing research papers
- Attention to using the Internet as a resource
- Reproduction of works of literature and art for analysis and writing

For assistance with *Writing About the Humanities* I would like to thank my colleague Janetta Rebold Benton, coauthor of *Arts and Culture: An Introduction to the Humanities,* for which this book has been designed as a companion. Thanks to Bud Therien, Publisher of Prentice-Hall Humanities, for sponsoring the book and supporting it.

Finally, I would like to thank my wife and best friend, Mary Hammond DiYanni, whose loving support continues to mean more to me than anything. And I wish to acknowledge the book's dedicatees, men whose respect for books and whose love of the arts are supremely evident in all they do.

Robert DiYanni

WRITING ABOUT

THE

HUMANITIES

THE

HUMANITIES

1
An Approach to Writing About the Humanities

Why write about works of art? For these reasons at least: first, because writing about a work of art leads us to read, observe, or listen to it more attentively, to notice characteristics about it we might overlook in a more casual reading, looking, or hearing. Second, because writing about works of art stimulates us to think about them. Putting words on paper provokes thought, gets our minds into gear. Third, we may wish to clarify our *feeling* about a work of art, as well as our *thinking*. We may wish to express what a particular work of art prompts us to think or feel, perhaps to endorse the ideas it conveys, perhaps to take exception to its subject, form, or execution. Writing about a work of art empowers us by allowing us to absorb it into our knowledge and experience.

This chapter presents an approach to works of art and ways to write about them. It encourages you to ask questions about the works you read, look at, and listen to—different kinds of questions, which lead to different kinds of responses. Three types of questions are essential:

- Questions that invite your *reaction* to the works you read, view, or hear
- Questions that encourage you to *interpret* those works
- Questions that require you to *evaluate* them

These types of questions and their associated forms of response lead to three ways of writing about works of art:

- Writing to understand works of art
- Writing to explain works of art
- Writing to evaluate works of art

In writing to understand works of art we are concerned primarily with how to make sense of them for ourselves. Our emphasis is on responding to the works emotionally as well as acquiring some sense of their qualities and power. The kind of writing associated with these goals is exploratory, and may assume the forms of freewriting, annotating, listing, and making notes.

In writing to explain works of art, we are concerned largely with interpretation, with making inferences based on our observations about artworks. (An inference is a statement about the unknown that is based on the known or the observed.) This type of writing to explain is more formal than the informal types of writing you do to understand a work of art for yourself. It is also more explanatory than exploratory.

In writing to evaluate works of art, we are concerned primarily with considering their value and their values. We make judgments about their quality, measuring them against aesthetic criteria and considering the social, moral, and cultural values they reflect, display, or endorse. Our emphasis in writing to evaluate is to arrive at conclusions about how we value works of art and why we value them as we do.

RESPONDING

When we listen to a song, watch a film, look at a photograph or painting, read a poem or story, or view a sunset, something happens to us. We feel something. Our emotions are stirred. Our thoughts are stimulated. In short, we react.

Consider, for example, a recent occasion when you did one of these things. Can you describe what you felt? Can you explain what it was about listening to that song, reading that poem or story, seeing that painting, watching that movie that moved you to feel what you did, that stimulated you to begin thinking? Think of some text, some work of music, literature, art, or film to which you responded strongly—one that made you think or feel deeply. Most likely that work, whatever it was, has become part of you. It has become what we might call an "identity touchstone," because it expresses something important to you as an individual. In some personal and powerful way, you have made that work your own.

Interestingly enough, you may very likely discover that others have made that same work or text their own—even though they may not have responded to it exactly as you did, though they may have seen in it things other than those you saw. Regardless of how others view this work or what they make of it as they appropriate it for their own identity, you have probably made it a part of your own inner life. In fact, depending upon how powerfully you were affected, the particular work you have identified may have been for you a door opening out to other experiences or kinds of knowledge. Or to change our image, it may have provided a key to unlock your understanding of the world, other people, or yourself. It may have provided you with a standard by which to judge other similar works or a frame through which you perceive and understand your experience.

Now think of some text or work that, upon first encounter, you didn't understand. Perhaps it was a painting you looked at or a poem or novel you read. Perhaps it was a song whose lyrics puzzled you or a film you couldn't make much sense of. You may have dismissed it as boring or stupid or meaningless. And perhaps, for you at the time, it was. Or you may have felt that there was indeed something to the work, even though you had trouble figuring it out. Such a questioning of your response is healthy and valuable, primarily because it starts you thinking about both the text and your reactions to it. On one hand, it invites you to reflect on yourself, on why you didn't like or understand the work. On the other hand, it may lead you back to take another look, to reconsider what you read, saw, or heard.

On those occasions when you are moved by a work, when it makes a strong impression on you, one that is meaningful, you begin to live with that work and let it live in you. You may begin to engage in a dialogue with the work so that it may affect how you think and see, and even live.

To respond fully to any work of art, we have to invest ourselves in it. We have to immerse ourselves in it, give it time to work on us, speak to us, engage our hearts and minds. When this happens, we will have made our study of texts more than a mere academic exercise. We will have made it something that matters in our lives.

Vincent van Gogh, *The Starry Night,* 1889, oil on canvas, 28¾ × 36½″ (73.7 × 92.1 cm). The Museum of Modern Art, New York.

Responding to a Painting: Vincent van Gogh's *Starry Night*

Look at the reproduction of Vincent van Gogh's painting *The Starry Night.* Spend a few minutes with the reproduction and write brief answers to the following questions:

1. What was your *first* reaction on seeing this work here? Why do you think you reacted this way?

2. What do you find most striking about the painting? What observations can you make about it?

3. What is your overall impression of the painting? Which of the following best describe your sense of it: calm, peaceful, energetic, frenzied, intense, casual, comfortable, feverish, photographic, visionary? Why do you have the impression you do? Can you think of other adjectives that better suit your impression of the work?

4. If you have access to a color reproduction, how do you react to van Gogh's colors? Consider the colors of the various stars, of the moon, of the sky, of the cypress tree that dominates the left foreground of the picture.

5. How do you react to van Gogh's swirling, sweeping, circular lines? to the thickness of his brush strokes? to the relationship in size and color between the depiction of nature above and town below?

6. How do you respond to van Gogh's departures from reality in the details of the painting. Would you prefer a painting of stars and moon and sky that more closely resembled a photograph? Why or why not?

WRITING EXERCISES

1. Using the previous set of questions, formulate a response to van Gogh's *Starry Night*. Write freely about what you notice, about how you feel, and about what you think. A couple of paragraphs will do.

2. Van Gogh's *Starry Night* has inspired many poems. Here is one by the contemporary American poet, Anne Sexton, on whom van Gogh's painting made a strong impression. Read Sexton's poem a few times, and then jot down a few sentences revealing your response to it.

Responding to Poem: Anne Sexton's "Starry Night"

That does not keep me from having a terrible
need of—shall I say the word—religion. Then I
go out at night to paint the stars.
　　—Vincent van Gogh in a letter to his brother

The town does not exist
except where one black-haired tree slips
up like a drowned woman into the hot sky.
The town is silent. The night boils with eleven stars.
Oh starry starry night! This is how
I want to die.

It moves. They are all alive.
Even the moon bulges in its orange irons
to push children, like a god, from its eye.
The old unseen serpent swallows up the stars.
Oh starry starry night! This is how
I want to die:

into that rushing beast of the night,
sucked up by that great dragon, to split
from my life with no flag,
no belly,
no cry.

Here are a few questions to guide your thinking about Sexton's poem.

1. Look first at the epigraph Sexton includes with her poem. To what extent does van Gogh's comment suggest why he painted the stars? How did the act of painting them affect van Gogh?

2. What does Sexton emphasize in her first stanza? What comparison does she make? What contrast does she identify in the painting? What personal statement does the speaker of the poem make?

3. What seems to be the emphasis of the second stanza? What impression of the sky does this stanza suggest to you? Why?

4. What do you make of the last five lines, which are really a continuation of the second stanza?

5. What does your reading of Sexton's poem add to your experience of van Gogh's painting? Does it alter your perception of it in any way? Do you see things you didn't notice before? Or do you see them another way?

6. Does Sexton's poem affect your response to the painting? Why or why not?

Even though you probably do not see van Gogh's *Starry Night* the way Anne Sexton does or make the same sense of it as she does, by looking at her poem carefully and considering its relationship to van Gogh's painting, you can understand her response. Her view of the painting, what she notices about it, and how she interprets it (the black-haired tree, the hot sky, and the dragon in the sky, for example) may enable us to see things in the painting we had not at first noticed ourselves. This does not mean, however, that we accept Sexton's view of the painting. Nor does it mean that we accept the speaker's apparent death wish.

The Starry Night in Context

You have been looking at one work of art, van Gogh's *Starry Night,* in the context of another: Sexton's poem about van Gogh. Now consider how a self-portrait by the painter, shown opposite, and an excerpt from a letter he wrote to his brother, Theo, shed light on *The Starry Night.*
Here are a few questions to prompt your thinking:

1. What do you notice about the background of the self-portrait? What do you notice about the way van Gogh painted his clothing?

2. How would you describe his face? Consider the eyes, nose, mouth.

Vincent van Gogh, *Self-Portrait,* Saint-Rémy, September 1889, oil on canvas, 25½ × 21½″ (65 × 54 cm). Musée d' Orsay, Paris.

3. What else do you find noteworthy about the self-portrait?

4. What connections can you make between the two paintings?

Here is the excerpt from van Gogh's letter to his brother, Theo:

For my own part, I declare I know nothing whatever about it; but to look at the stars always makes me dream as simply as I dream over the black dots of a map representing towns and villages. Why, I ask myself, should not the shining dots of the sky not be as accessible as the black dots on the map of France? . . .

I go out at night to paint the stars, and I dream always of a picture like of the house this with a group of living figures. . . .

These colours give me extraordinary exaltation. I have no thought of fatigue. . . . I have a terrible lucidity at moments when nature is so beautiful; I am not conscious of myself any more, and the pictures come to me as in a dream. . . .

Ah! portraiture, portraiture with the thought, the soul of the model in it. That is what I think must come.

WRITING EXERCISE

Write another paragraph or two about *The Starry Night,* incorporating what you learned from either the self-portrait, the letter excerpt, or both.

Responding to Whitman's "When I Heard the Learn'd Astronomer"

In the same way that you have been responding to van Gogh's painting, by considering its visual details and reacting to its elements, so, too, can you respond to the language and details of a work in writing such as a novel, play, or poem. In the following poem, Walt Whitman describes the reaction of a person (the poem's speaker) listening to an astronomy lecture. Whitman also hints at the speaker's response to actually looking at stars in the night sky. As you read, consider why the speaker responds the way he does, and how you yourself might respond, or perhaps have responded, in a similar situation.

When I Heard the Learn'd Astronomer

When I heard the learn'd astronomer,
When the proofs, the figures, were ranged in columns before me,
When I was shown the charts and diagrams, to add, divide, and measure
    them,
When I sitting heard the astronomer where he lectured with much
    applause in the lecture room,
How soon unaccountable I became tired and sick,
Till rising and gliding out I wander'd off by myself,
In the mystical moist night-air, and from time to time,
Look'd up in perfect silence at the stars.

1. Write a paragraph in response to Whitman's poem. Have you ever had an experience similar to the one Whitman describes in the first stanza? Have you ever felt "tired and sick" while listening to a lecture and wanted to get up and walk out? What did you do? Why?

2. Characterize the experience of the stars the speaker describes at the end of the poem. Have you ever stood out on a clear night and simply looked at the stars? Why? What was it like?

INTERPRETING

In the previous section on responding, the emphasis was on your feelings and personal response to works of art; here it will be on your thoughts, on your ideas about them. In that section you were encouraged to be subjective and impressionistic. In this section on interpreting, you will be asked to be more objective and analytical. Instead of eliciting your responses and feelings, you are now urged to think about the author's or artist's ideas and your own understanding of the works you see, read, and hear. The concern here is with interpretation.

When we interpret, we seek the artist's or author's view rather than our own; we ask what the work means, what it suggests rather than how it affects us. Interpretation aims at understanding, at intellectual comprehension rather than the emotional apprehension of responding. Thus you will now be shifting gears—moving beyond an informal and personal account of works and world to a more formal and public consideration of their significance.

But what is interpretation? And how do we actively engage in the process? Essentially, interpretation is making sense of something—a poem, a painting, a person, an event. We go about interpreting a work in the following way:

- We make *observations* about its details.
- We establish *connections* among our observations.
- We develop *inferences* (interpretive guesses) based on those connections.
- We formulate a *conclusion* based on our inferences.

To understand a work we need, first, to notice its details. You already began to do this in making observations about Vincent van Gogh's *Starry Night* and Walt Whitman's "When I Heard the Learn'd Astronomer." You need now to move beyond those more or less informal observations to a more careful and formal set of observations. This more formal way of making observations is associated with our analysis and interpretation.

To begin understanding any text or work, you must observe its details closely. In reading a story, for example, we notice details of time, place, and action. We attend to dialogue and action, noticing not only what characters say and do, but their manner of speaking and acting as well. In listening to a musical work, we attend to its melody and harmony, its instrumentation, its changes of tempo and dynamics (its loudness or softness). In looking at a painting or photograph, we observe the size, shape, and color of its figures. We notice their relative positions in foreground or background. We pay attention to shape, line, color, brushstroke. We attend, in short, to a work's elements or characteristic features.

But it's not enough simply to notice such things. That's only the first step. We must push on to establish connections and discover patterns among the observations we make.

Interpreting van Gogh's *Starry Night*

In viewing van Gogh's *Starry Night,* for example, you almost certainly noticed the intensity of its colors and the thickness of its brushstrokes. You may also have observed the way each star is surrounded by a circular burst of light. You probably realized, further, almost immediately upon seeing the picture, how it is not a realistic representation of the night sky, but rather the painter's expression of how he perceived the stars in the night, and perhaps how he felt about them. We could go on and list other observations about the work's details. But our point is simply that we do not observe these or any details in a vacuum. We seek to relate a work's details, to bring them together, to connect them into a coherent whole—and thus to make sense of the work as a whole.

To do that we have to literally "leap" to our third interpretive aspect: *inference*. There is no way around "the interpretive leap." We must make this inferential jump, even though it's risky, even though we may not be certain about our idea. But infer we must if we don't want to remain stuck with saying things like "I don't have any idea what this artist/writer is up to." So, then, what inferences are you willing to make about *The Starry Night?* How can you relate the details you noticed into a pattern that suggests a meaning?

Notice that you are asked to consider *a* meaning, not *the* meaning. Because works of art convey multiple meanings, there is no single, definitive, absolute, and final way to understand them. Your goal should be simply to develop the habits of mind that lead you to formulate your ideas and to engage in richly inferential thinking.

EXERCISE

Use the following questions to work toward interpreting Van Gogh's painting.

1. What do you think the painter may be expressing in *The Starry Night?* What attitudes, feelings, and ideas are communicated to you as you look at and think about it?

2. Think of other ways of "reading" the stars. How do astronomers read the stars? astrologers? sailors? lovers?

Once you begin making inferences about a work, you are actually already interpreting it. Although we usually reserve the word *interpretation* for a formal statement of the work's meaning, in a more general sense, your acts of observing and relating details about the painting are essentially interpretive. They are aspects of a single process—interpretation.

Interpretation requires you to take some intellectual risks. It invites you to speculate or wonder about the significance of an artwork's details. Remember that interpretation is not a science; it is, rather, an art that can be developed with practice.

Be aware as well that the four interpretive actions—making observations, establishing connections, developing inferences, and formulating conclusions—occur together and not in a series of neatly separated stages. Our acts of interpretation are continuous as we read, look, and listen. We don't delay making inferences, for example, until after we have made all our observations. Instead, we develop tentative conclusions *as* we read and observe, *while* we make connections and develop inferences. We may change and adjust our inferences and provisional conclusions both during our reading of a work and afterward, as we think back over it. We suspect that you will find yourself doing just that as you reread Whitman's poem.

Interpreting Walt Whitman's "When I Heard the Learn'd Astronomer"

You can follow the same procedure to interpret Whitman's "When I Heard the Learn'd Astronomer." To guide you through the process of interpretation, the following questions have been organized according to the interpretive steps outlined earlier—observing, connecting, inferring, and concluding. Use the questions to direct your rereading of Whitman's poem. Make notes either in the margins of this book or in another convenient place.

Making Observations

1. What do the following words have in common: *proofs, figures, columns, charts, diagrams, add, divide, measure?* Why is it important that these words occur in the first four lines but not in the last four lines of the poem?

2. How many sentences make up the poem? In how many stanzas is it cast? Why? If you were to split the poem into two sections, where would you break it? Why?

3. How many human figures are central to this poem? How many times does the poet use the word *I?* Why is it repeated?

Establishing Connections

4. What relationship exists between the first four lines and the last four lines of the poem? Can they be seen as representing a problem and its solution? a cause and its effects? Why?

5. What is the relationship between the words mentioned in question 1 and the following: "mystical moist night-air" and "perfect silence"?

6. Identify the relationship between each of the following pairs of details: the noise of the first four lines and the quiet of the last four; the speaker's sitting and his standing up and walking out; his being inside and outside; his being with others and his being alone. (By the way, can we be certain that the speaker is male? Is it important? Why or why not?)

Developing Inferences

7. What do you infer from the fact that the speaker gets up and walks out of the lecture room?

8. What do you infer from the applause the lecturer receives?

9. What do you infer about the speaker's experience as it is described in the last line?

Formulating a Conclusion

10. Would you say that this poem is about education? about different kinds of education? different ways of learning? If so, how would you characterize these ways of learning? If not, what is the poem about?

11. Is it a poem about nature? about our relationship with nature? about nature's effect on us? in what sense? Can the poem be "about" both education and nature—and other things as well?

WRITING EXERCISE

Write a couple of paragraphs formulating your interpretation of the poem. Identify an idea the poem suggests. You can use the ideas you discovered as you worked through the questions on observing, connecting, inferring, and formulating a conclusion.

Interpreting a Song: Franz Schubert's "Erlking"

Now that you've had a chance to put the interpretive process into action, consider a work in another medium—a song by the Austrian composer Franz Schubert (1797–1828). Schubert's "Erlkönig" (German for "erlking" or "elfking") is a *lied,* or song for voice with piano accompaniment. As the composer of the work, Franz Schubert wrote the music, but he did not write the lyrics. The verbal text of the song is a poem by the German poet Johann Wolfgang von Goethe (1749–1832).

Before listening to the music, read through the lyrics a few times. Consider the story the poem tells. Make sure you can identify the characters described and that you can follow what happens. Here, then, is the poem that Schubert set to music.

Erlkönig

Wer reitet so spät durch Nacht und Wind?
Es ist der Vater mit seinem Kind;
Er hat den Knaben wohl in dem Arm,
Er faßt ihn sicher, er hält ihn warm.

"Mein Sohn, was birgst du so bang dein
    Gesicht?"
"Siehst, Vater, du den Erlkönig nicht?
Den Erlenkönig mit Kron und Schweif?"
"Mein Sohn, es ist ein Nebelstreif."

"Du liebes Kind, komm, geh mit mir!
Gar schöne Spiele spiel ich mit dir;
Manch bunte Blumen sind an dem Strand,
Meine Mutter hat manch gülden Gewand."

"Mein Vater, mein Vater, und hörest du
    nicht,
Was Erlenkönig mir leise verspricht?"
"Sei ruhig, bleibe ruhig, mein Kind:
In dürren Blättern säuselt der Wind."

"Willst, feiner Knabe, du mit mir gehn?
Meine Töchter sollen dich warten schön;
Meine Töchter führen den nächtlichen Reihn
Und wiegen und tanzen und singen dich ein."

"Mein Vater, mein Vater, und siehst du nicht
    dort
Erlkönigs Töchter am düstern Ort?"
"Mein Sohn, mein Sohn, ich seh es genau:
Es scheinen die alten Weiden so grau."

"Ich liebe dich, mich reizt deine schöne
    Gestalt;
Und bist du nicht willig, so brauch ich
    Gewalt."
"Mein Vater, mein Vater, jetzt faßt er mich
    an!
Erlkönig hat mir ein Leid's getan!"—

Dem Vater grauset's, er reitet geschwind
Er hält in den Armen das ächzende Kind,
Erreicht den Hof mit Müh und Not;
In seinen Armen das Kind war tot.

The Erl-King

Who rides so late through the night and the
    wind?
It is the father with his child.
He holds the boy in his arm,
grasps him securely, keeps him warm.

"My son, why do you hide your face so
    anxiously?"
"Father, do you not see the Erl-King?
The Erl-King with his crown and tail?"
"My son, it is only a streak of mist."

"Darling child, come away with me!
I will play fine games with you.
Many gay flowers grow by the shore;
my mother has many golden robes."

"Father, father, do you not hear
what the Erl-King softly promises me?"
"Be calm, dear child, be calm—
the wind is rustling in the dry leaves."

"You beautiful boy, will you come with me?
My daughters will wait upon you.
My daughters lead the nightly round,
they will rock you, dance to you, sing you to
    sleep!"

"Father, father, do you not see
the Erl-King's daughters there, in that dark
    place?"
"My son, my son, I see it clearly:
it is the grey gleam of the old willow-trees."

"I love you, your beauty allures me,
and if you do not come willingly, I shall use
    force."
"Father, father, now he is seizing me!
The Erl-King has hurt me!"

Fear grips the father, he rides swiftly,
holding the moaning child in his arms;
with effort and toil he reaches the house—
the child in his arms was dead.

Earlier, when we looked at van Gogh's paintings *The Starry Night* and *Self-Portrait,* you were encouraged to pay attention to the thickness of van Gogh's brushstrokes and the vibrancy of his colors. As you listen to Franz Schubert's music, you should listen for different things. On first hearing, listen to the words and try to follow the story of the poem's action. You will be listening to a song sung in German. But you can follow along, listening to the German while reading the line-for-line English translation.

During this first hearing, you will also hear a piano accompaniment. In fact, the work begins with the piano as it introduces what becomes a dominant musical motif, or pattern of sound throughout the work. You can't miss it, as it is an insistent, repeated pattern of loud notes that Schubert uses to imitate the galloping of a horse. The horse is being ridden by a man who is carrying his young son with him as he rides. The poem/song describes how the son tells the father that the erlking is coming to take him away. The father thinks that the son is hallucinating and tries to console him. Upon reaching home, the boy dies in his father's arms.

Upon a second hearing, once you know the basic outline of the story the song describes, you can listen for the way the composer creates a series of different voices in the music. Even though there is only one singer, we have the sense that we are hearing four different voices: the father, the son, the erlking, and the narrator of the story. As you listen to the music, try especially to hear how the singer changes his voice to dramatize the differing voices of these four characters. We expect that you will hear how Schubert pitches the child's music higher than the music for the other characters.

You may also hear, perhaps on a third hearing, how the composer depicts the increasingly frantic nature of the child's desperation by raising the pitch of his voice each successive time he cries out to his father. As the song progresses, the composer makes the child's cries sound more helpless and desperate. The composer creates this effect by making the child's part a little louder, a bit more intense, and slightly higher in pitch each time.

On the third or perhaps even fourth hearing of the song, you may discover that the father's music is different from the child's. His melody is more controlled, less desperate, and more authoritative. The most beautiful melody of all, however, is that given to the erlking, who tries to enchant the child and snatch him away to fairyland. You may actually hear all of this on first or second hearing, but you will need a few additional hearings to sort out and really appreciate Schubert's musical accomplishment. You might also be interested to know as a sidelight that Schubert was only seventeen when he wrote this song, his first of more than six hundred, and one of his most highly regarded.

Through the musical means we have mentioned, and by means of others as well, which are too technical for our discussion here, Schubert accentuates the terror and pathos of Goethe's poem. By changing the music from stanza to stanza to reflect the developing dramatic action, Schubert brings out the emotion of the lyrics. One of his most successful musical enhancements occurs at the end. Following the abrupt termination of the piano's insistent rumbling is a dramatic pause between the words "In his arms the child" and the final words, "lay dead." It is a wonderfully expressive use of sound and silence.

WRITING EXERCISES

1. Select one of the songs on the tape, or one of your own favorites, and write an interpretation of it. Include in your discussion, as far as you are able, some attention to how the music brings out and accentuates the meaning of the words.

2. Go to the library and read about the life of Franz Schubert. If you have the time and inclination, see what you can find out about the legend of the erlking (a Danish legend, we understand). Or see what you can find out about the popularity of Schubert's song. Consider how your research enhances your understanding and appreciation of the song.

EVALUATING

In the previous sections, on responding and interpreting, you were encouraged to consider your personal responses and your understanding of different kinds of artworks. In doing so you were also (though perhaps without realizing it) assessing their values. You are now invited to focus specifically on the social, cultural, and moral concerns of some artworks. In doing so, you will begin to realize the importance of cultural attitudes, social conventions, and moral beliefs in the works we see, hear, and read.

What Is Evaluation?

But what is meant here by "evaluation"? Normally, when we speak of evaluation, we mean making a judgment about quality, about the success a particular work of art achieves—the artist's accomplishment or the work's expressive quality. Another way to think about evaluation, however, is as an appraisal or judgment of the cultural, moral, and aesthetic ideals that artworks reflect, support, or embody. This type of evaluation concerns a work of art's values, along with the values of the time and culture in which it was created, as well as the particular values we ourselves bring to our acts of evaluation.

In responding to and interpreting works of art, we bring to bear cultural, moral, and aesthetic beliefs. Our cultural values derive from our lives as members of families and societies. These values are affected by our race and gender, and also by the language we speak. Our moral values reflect our ethical norms—what we consider to be good and evil, right and wrong. These values are influenced by our religious beliefs and sometimes by our political convictions as well. Our aesthetic values determine what we see as beautiful or ugly, well or ill made.

Changing Values

Over time, with education and experience, our values often change. Through contact with other languages and cultures, we may come to understand the limiting perspective of our own. When we live with people other than our immediate families, for example, we may be persuaded to different ways of seeing many things we previously took for granted. Some of our beliefs, assumptions, and attitudes about religion, family, marriage, sex, love, school, work, money, and other aspects of life are almost sure to change.

As our lives and outlooks change, we may alter the way we view particular works. A film that we once admired for what it reveals about human behavior or one whose moral perspective impressed us may come to seem trivial or unimportant. On the other hand, we may find that a painting or a piece of music we once disliked later seems engaging and exciting. And just as individual tastes may change over time, so do cultural tastes in music, literature, art. Culture evolves; moral beliefs, aesthetic ideals, and social attitudes change.

Works of art themselves are intimately involved in such change. Works of art often, in fact, reflect or embody cultural changes, such as shifts in social attitudes, moral dispositions, and behavioral norms. In addition, works of art can also affect us and lead us to change our own perceptions, understanding, and perspective.

What we value in a particular work or how the works of particular artists and performers are valued in their time and later is largely a function of cultural and social attitudes, as well as of changing ideas about what is or is not considered acceptable or proper to a given art. In the same way that clothing styles change from decade to decade (and even from year to year) so, too, do musical and artistic styles—although not as rapidly. In popular music, for example, the music of Prince was once in fashion; so was the music of Pink Floyd and, further back, that of the Beach Boys. Today it may be Whitney Houston, Mariah Carey, or Garth Brooks who draws crowds of enthusiastic admirers. Once it was Frank Sinatra and Bing Crosby. You will see this in greater detail when you study the literature, music, or art of a country like France or a continent like Europe.

Similar fashions affect the fate of classical composers as well. Georg Friedrich Handel, whose *Messiah* is one of the most popular of classical choral compositions, was immensely popular. Handel's popularity, however, did not rest on works like *Messiah* (an oratorio that he had not yet written) but on his nearly forty operas in the Italian style—with each one more enthusiastically received than the one before—until Italian operas went out of fashion. Handel, a good businessman, reacted swiftly to the demise of Italian opera in his time by developing a new musical form, the oratorio, which became popular almost immediately. His operas have languished largely unperformed for more than two hundred years—until the past few years, when they have again been rediscovered. (*Messiah* continues to retain its appeal, even for many people who are not serious enthusiasts either of religion or of classical music.)

WRITING EXERCISES

Select one of the following questions and write a few paragraphs in response to it.

1. List three or four books you've read or films you've seen at different times in your life. Then select one and write a few paragraphs explaining how your later encounter with the book or film differed from your first reading or viewing.

2. Think about a television show or type of show (police drama, doctor or lawyer show, soap opera, family comedy) that you know. Discuss a few ways that the show's changes reflect the changing values of the times.

3. Identify a concert or theatrical production you attended that affected you or impressed you strongly. Consider why you were affected the way you were. Consider, also, whether your evaluation of the performance changed over time and, if so, why.

Considerations in Evaluation

When we evaluate artworks we consider the cultural assumptions, moral attitudes, and social convictions that animate them, especially in relationship to our own values. Our consideration may involve looking into the circumstances of their composition, the external facts and internal experiences of the artist's life, the attitudes and beliefs he or she may have expressed in letters or other comments. From even this brief list, we can see how complex evaluation can be.

Complicating matters even further is how we encounter the works we do. We come to paintings, poems, songs, and other works of art after many preliminary acts of evaluation by others. The artists who created them decided that they were valuable enough to preserve. The publishers who originally presented them to the public valued them, perhaps more for their potential profit than for the feelings, attitudes, ideas, or artistry they display. All who respond to works of art, whether teachers or students or the general public, will not value them the same way. Nor should they. Just as our personal responses to works of art and our interpretations of them differ, so, too, do our evaluations of them in terms of both their artistic success and their values.

Evaluation in Practice: Ernest Hemingway's Interchapter VII from *In Our Time*

We can clarify this discussion of evaluation with reference to a brief fictional piece that displays strong cultural dispositions and moral values. The text is a one-paragraph interchapter from Ernest Hemingway's fictional work *In Our Time.*

> While the bombardment was knocking the trench to pieces at Fossalta, he lay very flat and sweated and prayed oh jesus christ get me out of here. Dear jesus please get me out. Christ please please please christ. If you'll only keep me from getting killed I'll do anything you say. I believe in you and I'll tell every one in the world that you are the only one that matters. Please please dear jesus. The shelling moved further up the line. We went to work on the trench and in the morning the sun came up and the day was hot and muggy, and cheerful and quiet. The next night back at Mestre he did not tell the girl he went upstairs with at the Villa Rossa about Jesus. And he never told anybody.

Though brief, this text is rife with cultural attitudes and moral implications. It assumes a modest knowledge of war as it was fought in the early twentieth century—that we know, for example, what trenches are and what shelling is. It also assumes that we understand a soldier's going "up-stairs" with a "girl" at a place like the "Villa Rossa" (Red House).

The text, however, says little, if anything, directly—somewhat like the tight-lipped soldier who doesn't tell about his experience with the girl. What Hemingway's piece does is to work by implication, by suggestion concerning its three central topics: war, love, and religion. What Hemingway's text conveys it does largely by playing off conventional expectations about war, love, and religion. The soldier, for example, does not act heroically (as is the expectation). Instead, he cringes fearfully in the trenches. And he prays to God out of fear, trying to bargain with God, a bargain he winds up not keeping.

Our response to and evaluation of this soldier's language and behavior are influenced by our own cultural values and moral dispositions. Our evaluation of him turns on considerations such as whether we think he really believes in Jesus, and what such a belief might mean for him. It is affected by whether we think the soldier's prayer is "answered" by God in a possibly providential intervention to move the shelling "further up the line"—or whether you consider that a coincidence. Your judgment is also influenced by whether his going to a house of prostitution is something you understand or approve of—or not; and whether his not telling the girl or anybody else about Jesus is a serious violation of a solemn vow or, given the circumstances, excusable and perfectly understandable behavior.

Besides evaluating the behavior of the soldier, we also make judgments about the values we think the text espouses. Does the author seem to display sympathy for the soldier? Does Hemingway judge him harshly? The narrative voice is noncommittal, concerned more with portraying a situation than with commenting on it. This stance of objectivity is itself a "value," an attitude or disposition we must eventually assess, as we need to respond to the man's world depicted in the text, a world of war and violence, in which a woman (or "girl") figures only marginally, and then only as she is used by a soldier. In short, our sexual and social values, coupled with our religious beliefs and general cultural awareness, will strongly influence how we evaluate Hemingway's text.

WRITING EXERCISE

Select a work of art, music, or literature and write a short paper exploring its values.

THE HUMANITIES

2

An Overview of the Writing Process

Although we use the phrase "the writing process," there is no one single writing process that every writer uses all the time. Instead, there are many different writing processes—as many as there are people who write. Different writers follow a writing process in their own individual ways. Some writers produce many drafts; others, only a few. Some writers compose at the computer keyboard; others write first with pen on paper. Some writers write only in the morning; others, at night. Some writers require absolute silence; others need background music or conversation. You may prefer to write in your room or in the library, at a small desk or on a large table, with a portable computer, or on a desktop in the computer lab. Regardless of individual writing behaviors, writers confront common elements when they write.

All writers need to identify their topic and develop an idea about it. All writers need to create an organization that suits the evidence they use to develop and support their ideas. And all writers need to find a way to begin and end their writing, preferably in an engaging or memorable way. In working toward achieving these goals, writers typically follow an overall three-stage process consisting of prewriting, drafting, and revising. Two additional steps follow these stages: editing and proofreading.

PREWRITING

Prewriting refers to your preliminary efforts to do formal writing—the writing of essays and papers, reports and research projects. Prewriting strategies include making lists, jotting annotations, posing questions, and freewriting. We shall use the following sonnet by William Shakespeare (no. 73) to illustrate these prewriting strategies:

> That time of year thou may'st in me behold
> When yellow leaves, or none, or few, do hang
> Upon those boughs which shake against the cold,
> Bare ruined choirs where late the sweet birds sang.
> In me thou see'st the twilight of such day
> As after sunset fadeth in the west,
> Which by-and-by black night doth take away,
> Death's second self that seals up all in rest.
> In me thou see'st the glowing of such fire
> That on the ashes of his youth doth lie,
> As the deathbed whereon it must expire,
> Consumed with that which it was nourished by.
> > This thou perceiv'st, which makes thy love more strong,
> > To love that well which thou must leave ere long.

Making Lists

One of the simplest ways to prepare yourself to write is to list items that relate to the topic you will write about. If you are preparing to write an analysis of Shakespeare's sonnet "That time of year, thou may'st in me behold," you might list the details you observe during your readings of the poem. Your list might look something like this:

that time	me
yellow leaves	black night
no leaves	glowing fire
few leaves	ashes
cold	deathbed
bare boughs	ruined choirs

twilight   *sunset*

love   *youth*

Such a list can help you isolate particular kinds of details or images that the poem includes. You might notice, for example, that the poem includes images of time, of death, of cold and warmth. You might then divide your list of details and images into groups of similar kinds. Here is a list of details similar to the first one, but this time the images are grouped with others related to them.

yellow leaves	*twilight*	*cold*	*sunset*
few leaves	*sunset*	*ashes*	*glowing*
no leaves	*night*	*deathbed*	*nourished*
bare boughs		*consumed*	

This simple grouping of listed details helps you make connections better than the preliminary random list of observations. But this list, too, represents merely a place to begin thinking about your topic. As you think further about your subject, you should try to narrow your focus, to consider how details from your list might be used as evidence to support an interpretation of the poem.

Annotation

As an alternative to making a list, you might simply annotate Shakespeare's sonnet, making notes about your observations in the margins. When you annotate a text, you make brief notes about it, both in the margins and in the space above and below it—wherever you have room to write. You can also annotate within the text of the work by underlining and circling words and phrases, or bracketing words, phrases, lines, or stanzas.

Like making a list, writing annotations about a work offers a convenient and relatively painless way to begin writing about it. Annotating can get you started zeroing in on what you find interesting, engaging, or important about a work. You can also identify details you find confusing or puzzling. And your annotations can serve as starting points for thinking when it comes time to write a formal paper or report.

Here is an example of annotation applied to Shakespeare's sonnet:

autumn

That time of year thou may'st (in me) behold
When (yellow) leaves, or none, or few, do hang
Upon those boughs which shake against the cold, *tree limbs/choir stalls?*
Bare ruined choirs where late the sweet birds sang. | *1*

twilight
&
sunset
&
night

(In me) thou see'st the twilight of such day
As after sunset fadeth in the (west), ——> *fading sun = ? end of day —life*
Which by-and-by black night doth take away,
Death's second self that seals up all in (rest.) | *2*   *sleep = death*
(In me) thou see'st the glowing of such fire
That on the ashes of his youth doth lie,
As the deathbed whereon it must (expire,) —— *die [out] fire & life*

used —>
up

(Consumed) with that which it was nourished by. | *3*
This thou perceiv'st, which makes thy love more strong,
To love that well which thou must leave ere long.

Asking Questions

Another preliminary writing strategy is to ask yourself questions about your topic. Asking questions prompts thinking, because questions beg to be answered. Questions provoke thought; their very openness of form invites response. In the process of thinking about your subject, narrowing your focus, and considering evidence and examples you could use to support your ideas, you can ask yourself questions about the details and images you have listed and the connections you have been making among them. You can also ask yourself questions about your annotations, some of which may themselves be questions.

Questions can complicate your thinking, and thus move you beyond simply presenting information and offering easy explanations of facts. Here are a few questions you could ask yourself regarding Shakespeare's sonnet:

- What season is the poet/speaker describing?
- With what time of day is that season associated?
- Why does he say "in me" you can see that season?
- Why are the "choirs" "bare" and "ruined"?
- What is death's "second self"?
- What is described as fading?

- Who is dying?
- Who is speaking, who is spoken to, and what is their relationship?

EXERCISE

Choose a work of art. Annotate it, list your observations about it, and ask yourself some questions about it.

Focused Freewriting

Like the other techniques of prewriting described so far—listing, annotating, and questioning—focused freewriting is a form of preliminary writing for yourself, rather than a type of writing you do for others. Like those other kinds of prewriting, focused freewriting can help you generate ideas and get started thinking and writing about a work of art without your having to worry yet about how to organize your ideas or how to provide evidence to support them.

Focused freewriting is writing that is unstructured and unplanned, although it is centered on a single topic. When you freewrite around a central topic, such as the images in a poem, you jot down the first thoughts that come into your head, without worrying about where your thinking might lead you. One of the goals of freewriting, in fact, is to find out where this form of relaxed thinking and writing takes you.

When you freewrite, you do not worry about organization or grammar or punctuation. You try to write quickly—partly to free up your unconscious and partly to make the task of writing easier. Writing freely in this way breaks down inhibitions and releases intellectual energy that enables you to get some thoughts on paper or screen, thoughts you can later develop and analyze in more formal kinds of writing.

Freewriting is useful for many kinds of writing assignments. It is often a good way to begin simply because it is writing that you do for yourself, rather than writing that you will show to an audience—a teacher or classmates, for example. In this respect, freewriting frees you of the responsibility to be correct, to be profound, even to be interesting—except to yourself.

You can use freewriting in conjunction with other prewriting techniques, such as making lists and asking questions. One way to do this is to select one of the more interesting (to you) items on your list or from your annotations and begin freewriting about it. Another is to take a couple of your more provocative questions and begin answering them in freewriting.

Here is an example of freewriting about Shakespeare's sonnet:

Freewriting Sample

> *That time of year—what time—autumn when leaves fall. Speaker compares himself to season. Poem turns on idea of seasons of life. Then shift to day/night.*
>
> *Does night or twilight = Fall? Day = Life; Night = Death. Fire is Life; Ashes death. Puzzling line about fire consumed what it's nourished by.*
>
> *Poem set up as sonnet—14 lines; rhymes; 4-line sections + rhyming conclusion—couplet.*
>
> *Meaning of conclusion?? We love things we are soon to lose. We love them more because we have them only a little while longer??*
>
> *Lots of images—details about day and night— fire and burning and going out—birds and leaves and trees. Figure out section by section how images work to convey ideas.*

In this example the writer jots down thoughts as they come. Ideas are hinted at rather than developed. Overall, the freewriting lacks focus but includes some promising leads for the writer to explore. When you use freewriting as a preliminary strategy, be sure that you do it more than once. Use your initial freewriting to see where your mind takes you with the topic. Use later freewriting to focus on one or another aspect, issue, or question raised in your earlier freewriting.

EXERCISES

1. Do some focused freewriting on a work you expect to write about or have been assigned to write about. Start your freewriting by considering an item from one of your lists, annotations, or questions.

2. What did you discover from your freewriting? To what extent did you think of things while you were writing that you didn't realize you were going to write? To what extent did you write some things that you didn't know you knew? To what extent did you find yourself getting into a rhythm, coming up with ideas, examples, and perspectives to express about the topic?

Summarizing and Analyzing

As a step toward more formal academic writing or preparing a paper or report on a humanities topic, you may need to summarize the gist or central idea of a written text or work. A summary provides an interpretation or explanation in your own words of a work's themes or a writer's central idea in a work. A succinct account of a work, a summary condenses or compresses its thought.

Writing a summary requires careful reading, in part to assure that you understand the work you are summarizing. Writing a summary helps you analyze because it requires that you consider carefully a work's details and structure. Writing a summary requires essentially two kinds of skills: identifying the central idea of the work you are summarizing and recognizing the evidence that supports that idea. In writing a summary, you build on the observations, connections, and inferences you make while reading a literary, philosophical, or historical text; observing a work of painting, sculpture, or architecture; or listening to a work of music.

A summary differs from an analysis in that analysis presents the evidence for the writer's ideas whereas a summary, most often, simply expresses the central idea of the work of art without providing the evidence. Frequently, summary and analysis are woven together in academic writing about the humanities. Consider the following example, a brief summary and analysis of the imagery in Shakespeare's sonnet:

Sample Summary and Analysis

> Perhaps the first thing to mention about the metaphorical language of the sonnet is that its central images appeal to three senses: sight, hearing, and touch. The images of the first four lines include appeals to each of these senses: we <u>see</u> the yellow leaves and bare branches; we <u>feel</u> the cold that shakes the boughs; we <u>hear</u> (in imagination) the singing birds of summer.
>
> These images collectively become metaphors, ways of talking about one thing in terms of something else. Autumn, for example, is "that time of year" when leaves turn yellow and tree branches become bare of leaves. Shakespeare compares the barren branches to an empty choir loft because the chorus of singing birds has departed with the

coming of colder weather. And because Shakespeare's speaker says that "you" (we) can behold autumn <u>in him</u>, we realize that he is talking about aging in terms of the seasons.

In lines 5-8 the metaphor of autumnal aging gives way to another: that of twilight ending the day. These lines describe the setting of the sun and the coming on of night. The emphasis here is on "black" night taking away the light of the sun; the sun's setting is seen as a dying of its light. The implied comparison of night with death is directly stated in line 8, where night is described as "death's second self." Like death, night "seals up all in rest." But while night's rest is temporary, the rest of death is final.

These metaphors of autumn and evening emphasize the way death comes on gradually. Autumn precedes winter and twilight precedes night just as illness precedes death. The poem's speaker knows that he is in the autumn of his life, the twilight of his time. This metaphor is continued in a third image in lines 9-12 of the sonnet: the dying of the fire, which in its dying out of light and heat symbolizes the dying out of the speaker's life. In addition, the speaker's youth is compared with "ashes," which serve as the "deathbed" on which he will "expire."

Literally, these lines say that the fire will expire as it burns up the fuel that feeds it. In doing so, the fire glows with light and heat. The glowing fire then becomes a metaphor for the speaker's life, which is still "glowing," but which is beginning to die out as it consumes itself. Like the dying fire, the speaker's youth has turned to ashes. Also like the dying fire, the speaker's life is "consumed with that which it was nourished by." Literally, the fire consumes itself by burning up the logs that fuel it. The fire, like the speaker's life, in its very glowing burns towards its own extinction.

WRITING (DRAFTING)

Once you have done some prewriting you are ready to write a draft, or first attempt, at your essay, paper, or report. When you draft a piece of writing, you do so fully aware that you will have an opportunity to revise, to make changes later. This is important so that you do not worry about trying to achieve perfection with your first draft. First drafts tend to be rough drafts, even though you may have employed one or more prewriting strategies to help you get started writing. Writing a first full draft, however rough, enables you to acquire an overview of what you want to say, what you want to include in your writing. Even though your sense of what will be included may change when you revise, it is helpful to try to generate in your first draft an overview of the writing as you envision it from beginning to end.

The Purpose of Drafting

The purpose of this draft is simply to write down your ideas and to see how they can be developed and supported. Think of the rough draft as an opportunity to discover what you think about the subject and to test and refine your ideas. Don't worry about having a clearly defined thesis or main idea in mind before beginning your draft. Instead, use your first draft to discover an idea, to clarify your thinking.

In drafting your paper, consider your purpose. Are you writing to provide information and make observations about a work, a philosophical idea, a historical event? Are you writing to argue for a particular way to interpret it? Ultimately, all explanations are interpretations, and all interpretations are forms of argument; that is, interpretive explanations are persuasive attempts to convince others to see things the way you do. In developing your draft of an interpretive explanation, you will be arguing for the validity of your way of seeing, not necessarily to the exclusion of all other ways, but to demonstrate that your understanding of the work, idea, or event is reasonable and valuable.

Your draft provides an occasion for you to identify your central idea or thesis and to provide evidence in its support. Your evidence may take the form of examples, facts, statistics, quotations from authoritative sources, personal stories, and other forms of information. Try to be as specific as you can in both identifying your central idea and in providing particulars to make it clear and interesting to your readers.

Moreover, since your readers will respond as much to how you support your arguments as to your ideas themselves, you will need to concentrate on providing evidence for your thinking carefully and thoroughly.

Most often this evidence will take the form of observations you make about the work, idea, or event. Additional evidence may come from secondary sources, from the comments of experienced observers, whose interpretations may influence and support your own thinking.

In marshalling evidence for your ideas from your observations about the work itself and from the views of others, keep the following guidelines in mind.

- Be fair minded. Try to avoid oversimplifying or distorting either the work or what others have written about it.
- Be cautious. Qualify your claims. Limit your discussion to what you can confidently demonstrate.
- Be logical. See that the various elements of your argument fit together and that one part of your discussion does not contradict another part.
- Be accurate. Present facts, details, and quotations correctly.
- Be confident. Believe in your ideas and present them with conviction.

One last point about drafting—try to write your first draft quickly. If you get stuck in the midst of your draft, leave some blank space and skip ahead to a part that you find easier to write. You can return to the spaces while completing your first draft, or you can fill them in when you revise.

Organizing Your Draft

Another important aspect of your draft is organization. You need not worry about this too much at first, but you should have some sense of what to begin with, how to conclude, and how to shape the evidence you include in the middle sections of your essay, paper, or report. You will be able to make adjustments in your organization when you revise. But it is important to have an overall sense of how your writing is unfolding even in the first draft.

As you organize your writing, try to envision it as a three-part structure with a beginning, a middle, and an ending. The beginning introduces your central idea or your thesis. The middle presents evidence and develops your idea. The ending provides a perspective on your idea and reminds readers of your supporting evidence.

The beginning or introduction leads your readers into your writing. The ending leads them out of it. These parts are relatively short in comparison to the middle, which includes the explanations, examples, and evidence to support your ideas. It is this larger and more complex middle part that you need to think about from the standpoint of organization.

If your writing requires (or if you decide to provide) historical background for your topic, for example, you will need to decide whether to put that background all in one place or to spread it throughout your essay, paper, or report. Should you present your most important and interesting examples and evidence first or last? If you have three or four aspects of your subject to discuss, should you begin with the easiest or least complex first, or might you want to put that aspect in the middle or at the end, just before your conclusion? If you begin with one rather than another aspect of your subject, will that make it easier or more difficult for you to move to the others?

Among the more common strategies for organizing writing are the order of importance (climactic order) and the order of time sequence (chronological order). In climactic order, you present your least important or complex ideas, examples, and evidence first and your most important or complex ideas, examples, and evidence last. In chronological order, you present events and ideas in the sequence in which they developed or the order in which they actually occurred.

REVISING

Once you have written a full first draft, however rough, you are ready to revise. Ideally, you should leave some time between your first draft and your revision. Get away from your draft awhile—at least overnight, if possible, preferably even longer.

Revision is not something that occurs only once, at the end of the writing process. Redrafting your essay, paper, or report to consider the ordering of paragraphs and the use of examples is one significant approach to revision. Other aspects of revision involve conceptual, organizational, and stylistic issues.

Conceptual revision involves reconsidering your central idea or thesis. As you write a first or even a second draft, your understanding of your topic and what you want to say about it may change. You might decide that your original idea is too simple, too vague, or simply unconvincing. You may end up discarding that idea and substituting something else in its place. In working through your first draft, you might actually change your mind about your idea and reverse the direction of your thinking.

Organizational or structural revision involves asking yourself whether the arrangement that you used in your first draft best presents your present line of thought. Is your organizational framework clear? Does it make sense? Does your introduction clarify your topic and state your idea? Do your supporting details provide evidence in a way that is both sensible to you and should be clear and persuasive to your readers? Does your conclusion follow logically from the unfolding of your idea in the middle?

You can use the following questions as guidelines for revising:

Revision Guidelines

- To what extent are you satisfied with your idea, with your thesis as it is currently formulated? How might you change it to make it more accurate, more complex, and more interesting?
- Are you satisfied with your organization? To what extent can you identify the overall organizational plan of your essay? Where does its beginning end? Where does the ending begin? And how is the middle set up, arranged, organized?
- To what extent are your sentences concise and clear? Can you eliminate words without altering your meaning?
- To what extent have you maintained a consistent tone? If your tone shifts at one point or another, was this by design, or was it an accident?
- How can you determine whether your level of language—your word choice, sentence structure, idiom, and tone—is appropriate for your topic and your audience?

EDITING

When you edit your completed revised draft, you should look for errors in grammar, spelling, usage, mechanics, and punctuation. Your guide to these matters should be a current college handbook, most likely one that has been assigned or required for one of your English courses.

Editing Guidelines

- How can you check for grammatical errors: inconsistencies in verb tenses and problems with subject-verb agreement, pronoun-antecedent agreement, sentence fragments, comma splices, and the like?
- To what extent do you need to check on tricky verbs such as *lie* and *lay,* on questions of usage concerning *who* and *whom,* on aspects of mechanics such as the use of capitalization and italics?
- Why might it be necessary for you to check for errors in spelling or punctuation? How should you go about this checking?

PROOFREADING

As a final step, proofread your writing. When you proofread, you should look to see that you have made the kinds of corrections necessary during the editing stage. If you notice that you need to correct a spelling error or that you need to add a punctuation mark, you can do so in black ink. (You need not print out an entire copy again because of a few minor mistakes.) You can even add missing words, such as *a* or *the,* for example.

You can use the following guidelines to help you proofread carefully:

Proofreading Guidelines

- Read the final draft aloud to hear mistakes.
- Read your final edited draft one line at a time, focusing on individual words and sentences, rather than on your ideas and examples.
- Read some paragraphs backward, last sentence first.
- Look for omitted words in sentences and omitted letters in words.
- If you discover too many mistakes requiring correction, retype individual pages—or the entire paper—as necessary.

Finally, make a copy for your instructor and an extra copy for yourself, in case your work is mislaid. An extra hard copy may also be needed if your computer hard drive malfunctions or if the file on your floppy disk is accidentally erased.

CONSIDERING PURPOSE
AND AUDIENCE

Much of what you say, and especially the way you choose to say it, depends on your purpose or aim in writing, and on an understanding of your audience. If, for example, your purpose is to summarize the artistic achievements of the ancient Greeks, you will write an explanatory paper that provides many examples of their numerous artistic, literary, and political achievements. If you are writing to analyze the development of a particular style of Hellenistic architecture or sculpture, you would provide more analysis and less information, and your analytical approach would be deep rather than wide. If, however, you were writing, instead, to evaluate the influence of ancient Greek cultural achievements or to challenge a common view of their importance or influence, you would develop a more argumentative piece of writing, one heavier on providing evidence for the claims you would make.

Similar considerations will affect your writing for differing audiences. For example, the extent to which your audience shares a common basis of information or expertise should govern the extent to which you use technical language in an essay, paper, or report. The type of audience you are writing for will affect the amount of detail you include, the kinds of examples you use to illustrate and explain your ideas, and the amount of background or contextual information you decide to provide. In writing for students in your introductory humanities class, with a variety of different majors, interests, and backgrounds, you could not write about a technical aspect of a subject—poetic meter, for example—in the same way you could for students in an advanced poetry course. The more advanced students of poetry would be presumed to possess the technical understanding of poetic meter that others could not be expected to have. As a result, you would make different decisions about language and context in writing about the same subject for those two different audiences.

As a writer, you should always consider what your audience needs to know to understand your ideas. Thinking about your audience's needs will increase your chances of interesting them in your writing, as well as ensuring that they understand and appreciate your ideas. You can use the following questions as guidelines to help you remember to consider your audience when you write:

Audience Guidelines

- Who are my readers? Are they "experts" in the subject I am writing about? Or are they "generalist" nonexpert readers?
- What assumptions can I make about my audience?
- What response can I reasonably expect from my audience? Why?
- To what extent is my topic or idea something my audience may disagree with? What can I do to win the audience over?
- What is the most appropriate tone to use when writing for this audience?

CONSIDERING TONE

You don't write the same way for all readers in all situations. You adjust your tone—your attitude toward the subject as expressed by the style you use and the writerly decisions you make. You establish the tone of your writing according to your purpose or reasons for writing and the audience for whom you are writing.

Academic writing—the writing you do for your college courses—will often require a formal tone, like the tone established by environmental historian William Cronon in the passage quoted on pages 35–36. This is so because your instructors consider the essays, papers, reports, and research projects you produce to be serious intellectual efforts. You will attempt to demonstrate in your writing that you can use the language of the discipline—of literature or art history, for example—to analyze and explain, to inform and persuade your readers about an idea you have concerning an interesting issue or an important topic.

The tone of academic writing will almost always require you to be reasonable and objective, serious and thoughtful. These qualities are typically valued in such writing. Your purpose in academic writing is less to entertain than to explain and analyze, thereby demonstrating your command of ideas.

Just because academic writing avoids casual forms of expression does not mean that it must be dull or uninteresting. Despite its formality, academic writing can accommodate wit and humor as well as personal experience, engaging stories, and surprising details. Your tone in all the writing you do for your college courses will depend in part on your subject, and in part on your purpose in writing, as well as on your sense of what is appropriate for your audience—typically, your instructor and your classmates.

What follows are excerpts that illustrate variations in tone achieved with differences in word choice, sentence structure, idiom, and organization. Following each excerpt is a brief commentary that identifies the writer's tone and explains how it is achieved.

Here is a descriptive passage from an essay by Jane Brox about the influenza epidemic of 1918:

> In ordinary times, the bankers, lawyers, and mill owners who lived on Tower Hill opened their doors to a quiet broken only by the jostle of a laden milk wagon, the first stirrings of a wind in the elms, or the quavering notes of a sparrow. It was the height of country; the air, sweet and clear. Looking east from their porches they could survey miles of red-brick textile mills that banked the canals and the sluggish Merrimack, as well as the broad central plain mazed with tenements. To their west was a patchwork of small dairy holdings giving over to the blue distance. But for the thirty-one mornings of October 1918 those men adjusted gauze masks over their mouths and noses as they set out for work in the cold-tinged dawn, and they kept their eyes to the ground so as not to see what they couldn't help but hear: the clatter of motorcars and horse-drawn wagons over the paving stones, as day and night without ceasing the ambulances ran up the hill bringing sufferers from the heart of the city and the hearses carried them away.
>
> It had started as a seemingly common thing—what the linestorm season always brings, born on its wind and on our breath, something that would run its course in the comfort of camphor and bed rest. At first there had been no more than six or eight or ten cases a day reported in the city, and such

news hardly took up a side column in the papers, which were full of soldiers' obituaries and reports of a weakening Germany. As September wore on, however, the death notices of victims of the flu began to outnumber the casualties of war. Finally it laid low so many the Lawrence Board of Health set aside its usual work of granting permits to keep roosters, charting the milk supply, and inspecting tenements. The flu took up all its talk—how it was to be treated, how contained, how to stay ahead of the dead. The sufferers needed fresh air and isolation, and their care had to be consolidated to make the most of the scarce nurses and orderlies. So the board took a page from other stricken cities and voted to construct a makeshift tent hospital on their highest, most open land that offered the best air, which was the leeward side of Tower Hill where a farm still spread across the slope.

Comment

The style of this passage is notable for its long complex sentences laden with precisely evoked images. With a profusion of specific details, the writer recreates the time and place she describes: Lawrence, Massachusetts, in October 1918. Some of her longer sentences break in the middle, punctuated with semicolon or colon. Others make use of interrupting dashes that set up what comes after them. Throughout the passage, Brox sets her description of the action in a larger context—the context of "ordinary times" and the context of the first world war, with deaths from the flu outnumbering deaths from the war. The details in the first and last sentences of the passage convey a sense of quiet beauty that is violated by the deathly reality of the disease, which is recorded by the writer with controlled objectivity.

Brox writes as an essayist who uses detailed description in the service of local history. Her aim is to recreate the feeling of a particular place and time during the influenza epidemic of 1918, in much the same way historians like Barbara Tuchman in *A Distant Mirror* have recreated what it was like to live during the time when the Black Death (bubonic plague) raged during the European Middle Ages.

Here is a second example, this one from William Cronon on the idea of wilderness:

The time has come to rethink wilderness.

This will seem a heretical claim to many environmentalists, since the idea of wilderness has for decades been a fundamental tenet—indeed, a passion—of the environmental movement, especially in the United States. For many Americans wilderness stands as the last remaining place where civilization, that all too human disease, has not fully infected the earth. It is an island in the polluted sea of urban-industrial modernity, the one place we can turn for escape from our own too-muchness. Seen in this way, wilderness presents itself as the best antidote to our human selves, a refuge we must somehow recover if we hope to save the planet. As Henry David Thoreau once famously declared, "In Wildness is the preservation of the World."

But is it? The more one knows of its peculiar history, the more one realizes that wilderness is not quite what it seems. Far from being the one place on earth that stands apart from humanity, it is quite profoundly a human creation—indeed, the creation of very particular human cultures at very particular moments in human history. It is not a pristine sanctuary where the last remnant of an untouched, endangered, but still transcendent nature can for at least a little while longer be encountered without the contaminating taint of civilization. Instead, it is a product of that civilization, and could hardly be contaminated by the very stuff of which it is made. Wilderness hides its unnaturalness behind a mask that is all the more beguiling because it seems so natural. As we gaze into the mirror it holds up for us, we too easily imagine that what we behold is Nature when in fact we see the reflection of our own unexamined longings and desires. For this reason, we mistake ourselves when we suppose that wilderness can be the solution to our culture's problematic relationships with the nonhuman world, for wilderness is itself no small part of the problem.

Comment

Cronon's tone, although challenging, is nonetheless academic, in ways that Brox's tone in the influenza essay excerpt is not. Cronon introduces a quotation from Thoreau, a standard move in academic writing, and he also provides historical perspective, another common strategy.

Academic as well is the complex sentence structure Cronon employs, as is his use of qualification. Note, for example, how the qualifications he makes at the beginning of the third paragraph are especially well suited to the complexity of his idea. Moreover, Cronon's carefully controlled language creates an effect of a reasoned discourse in which an original idea is being thoughtfully considered. Cronon attempts to persuade through thoughtful analysis of a complex historical situation: the relation of human beings to their natural environment. Cronon makes his case tactfully but with a hint of warning.

THE AURAL/ORAL DIMENSION OF WRITING

Although we often read silently, it is beneficial on occasion to read some writing aloud. Poetry, of course, benefits from oral reading, from voicing the writer's words and lines the better to hear the sounds created in the poem—the sounds and rhythms that make it poetry, in fact. But prose, too, benefits from being heard aurally. By the way, the word used for speaking aloud is *oral* and for hearing what is read aloud *aural*. Every "oral" reading is also an "aural" one, even if the only one present is the reader who is reading aloud, for that reader is also a listener.

Why is it beneficial for a writer to read a draft of an essay, paper, or report aloud? The answer, quite simply, is that reading aloud slows things down. By slowing down, you can focus and concentrate more on the words and sentences of your writing and thus can better observe whether your words and sentences look and sound right. Another reason for reading your writing aloud is that in voicing your words you add an additional sense— the sense of hearing—to the one you use ordinarily when reading your writing: your sight. Adding hearing to seeing doubles the attention you give your writing and increases your chances of picking out places that need work. The ear often prompts the eye to see.

You can go even further with hearing your writing by reading your work aloud into a tape recorder. By doing that, you can concentrate during playback on the way your writing sounds. You can attend especially to the phrasing and the rhythm of your writing, as well as to meaning.

Still another way to use reading your writing aloud to advantage is to imagine yourself reading for an audience—or actually reading your writing to an audience, a few friends, classmates, or family members. Reading aloud for your audience will prompt you to emphasize certain words, phrases, sentences, or sections. Quite possibly, in reading your work aloud to different audiences, you might find yourself shifting the emphasis or reading with a different tone for each.

Adding the aural dimension to your writing can make you a more careful and attentive writer and also a more appreciative and observant reader of others' writing—if you are also willing to slow down and read aloud the work of others as well.

THE
HUMANITIES

3
Writing
a Comparison

In his book *The ABC of Reading,* the modernist poet Ezra Pound suggests that the best way to develop a critical aesthetic discrimination is to compare works of art rather than to analyze and evaluate them in isolation. "The proper method for studying poetry and good letters," Pound writes, "is the method of contemporary biologists, that is, careful firsthand examination of the matter, and continued comparison of one 'slide' or specimen with another." This chapter provides you with an opportunity to put Pound's advice to use by focusing on writing a comparative analysis.

As Pound suggests, you can gain a clearer and richer understanding of a work by comparing (and contrasting) it with another. Strictly speaking, comparison emphasizes similarities between works, whereas contrasts emphasize differences. In this chapter, however, comparison will be used in the broad sense, to include both similarities and differences.

THE PURPOSE AND VALUE
OF COMPARISON

It is important to note from the start that comparison is a strategy or a tool for analysis rather than an end in itself. Thus, when you engage in comparative analysis or evaluation of works of art, you do so with a purpose—

ultimately, to make an argument about the works. For example, you might wish to claim that one work is more complex than another, that it better illustrates a particular style, that it more fully reflects attitudes of the culture in which it was produced, or that it better represents an artist's or author's achievement. The point, simply, is that you use comparison as a way to analyze works of art so that you can explain your views of them more clearly and more cogently.

A second important matter of note is that comparison is also a strategy for thinking and a way of learning about works of art. For example, through doing a comparative analysis of two statues of David, one by Michelangelo and another by Bernini, you come to understand both sculptors' accomplishments better and you come to appreciate their sculptures more fully than if you were simply to analyze one without reference to the other. In addition, by being able to refer to both sculptures, you can present your observations and understanding of them in writing.

A third and final general point is that making comparisons is not merely an academic exercise. Art historians employ comparison when evaluating the authenticity of a work, such as a painting attributed to Rembrandt. They typically compare the attributed painting with some of his genuine works painted in the same medium at approximately the same time. Historians use comparison in examining the causes and effects of political developments and social change. And literary critics typically use comparison in evaluating novels, poems, and plays, sometimes by the same writer at different points in a career, other times by different authors writing similar kinds of works around the same time, possibly in the same country.

TWO WAYS OF ORGANIZING A COMPARATIVE ANALYSIS

In writing a comparative analysis, you can organize your paper or report in two ways. You can use what is known as the *block method,* or you can use the *alternating approach.* In the block method, you discuss one work in its entirety before taking up the other one. In other words, you present everything you have to say about each work separately—first one work and then the other.

In the alternating approach, you weave back and forth between the works, highlighting first one feature of each work, then moving on to discuss another. Throughout your paper, you would be discussing both works together with reference to each aspect under consideration—a building's structure, for example, or its style, or its size, materials, or color. Moreover, in the alternating approach, you can move back and forth in alternating paragraphs of an essay, or in alternating sentences in a paragraph.

One of these approaches is not inherently better than the other. In fact, writers typically use both ways of organizing a comparison together. In one part of an essay, for example, you might focus on each work in alternation and in another use the back-and-forth alternating approach. Here is a brief example of the block method used to compare the use of space in a typical American and a typical Chinese home:

> Americans have a sense of space, not of place. Go to an American home in exurbia, and almost the first thing you do is drift toward the picture window. How curious that the first compliment you pay your host inside his house is to say how lovely it is outside his house! He is pleased that you should admire his vistas. The distant horizon is not merely a line separating earth from sky, it is a symbol of the future. The American is not rooted in his place, however lovely: his eyes are drawn by the expanding space to a point on the horizon, which is his future. By contrast, consider the traditional Chinese home. Blank walls enclose it. Step behind the spirit wall and you are in a courtyard with perhaps a miniature garden around a corner. Once inside his private compound you are wrapped in an ambiance of calm beauty, an ordered world of buildings, pavement, rock, and decorative vegetation. But you have no distant view: nowhere does space open out before you. Raw nature in such a home is experienced only as weather, and the only open space is the sky above. The Chinese is rooted in his place. When he has to leave, it is not for the promised land on the terrestrial horizon, but for another world altogether along the vertical, religious axis of his imagination.
>
> —Yi-Fu Tuant, "American Space, Chinese Place"

Notice how Yi-Fu Tuant first describes the American home and its sense of space. Only when he finishes his comments about that does he introduce his ideas about Chinese conceptions of home and space. Notice, too, that the writer uses comparison to make a point: that the American conception of space differs dramatically from the Chinese concept of place. And, finally, notice that Tuant is less interested in the space inside the houses he describes. Rather, he makes his point by describing the relationship of outdoor spaces to the typical American and Chinese home.

By contrast, in the example that follows, the comparison is arranged alternatively. The literary critic George Steiner compares Homer's epic *The Iliad* with Tolstoy's novel *War and Peace*. The emphasis is on the Russian novel, which Steiner illuminates by invoking a series of comparisons with Homer's work—within the confines of a single paragraph.

And this is where it touches significantly on the art of Tolstoy. His also is an immanent realism, a world rooted in the veracity of our senses. From it God is strangely absent. In Chapter IV [of this book], I shall attempt to show that this absence can not only be reconciled to the religious purpose of Tolstoy's novels but that it is a hidden axiom of Tolstoyan Christianity. All that needs saying here is that there lies behind the literary techniques of the *Iliad* and of Tolstoy a comparable belief in the centrality of the human personage and in the enduring beauty of the natural world. In the case of *War and Peace* the analogy is even more decisive: where the *Iliad* evokes the laws of *Moira,* Tolstoy expounds his philosophy of history. In both works the chaotic individuality of battle stands for the larger randomness in men's lives. And if we consider *War and Peace* as being, in a genuine sense, a heroic epic it is because in it, as in the *Iliad,* war is portrayed in its glitter and joyous ferocity as well as in its pathos. No measure of Tolstoy pacifism can negate the ecstasy which young Rostov experiences as he charges down on the French stragglers. Finally, there is the fact that *War and Peace* tells of two nations, or rather of two worlds, engaged in mortal combat. This alone has led many of its readers, and led Tolstoy himself, to compare it with the *Iliad.*

—from *Tolstoy or Dostoevsky*

Steiner's paragraph is excerpted from a chapter in which he elaborates the comparison between Homer and Tolstoy in detail. In the paragraph quoted above, Steiner uses comparison of a single work by each writer to advance a number of claims about Tolstoy's novels. His first point is that God is mysteriously absent in Tolstoy's novels, especially in *War and Peace.* In place of God, Steiner claims that Tolstoy, like Homer, emphasizes the centrality of human experience and the enduring beauty of nature. Second, he compares Homer's use of *Moira,* or fate, with Tolstoy's use of a philosophy of history, suggesting that the two writers share a belief in the randomness, or accidental quality, of human life. Third, Steiner compares the two works in light of their concern for what he terms the "joyous ferocity" of war. And fourth, and finally, Steiner aligns the two works by virtue of their depiction of two worlds locked in "mortal combat."

Both Tuant and Steiner structure their comparisons in ways that allow them to express their ideas clearly and efficiently. Tuant's use of block structure in developing his comparison of the American and Chinese sense of space works very well for the contrast he develops. Steiner's use of an alternating structure in unfolding his comparison between Homer's epic and Tolstoy's novel is equally effective for his emphasis on similarities between the two works.

Whether you use the block method or the alternating structure in developing a particular comparison will depend on your purpose, the complexity of your subject, and the nature of your ideas. But keep the following considerations in mind as you use either or both of these techniques for comparative analysis:

- When you *alternate,* consider whether your readers stay with you as you zigzag back and forth between works you compare. Be sure to make the overall point of the back-and-forth comparative movement clear—perhaps in a concluding sentence (for a paragraph) or in a concluding paragraph (for an essay).

- When you use the *block* method, consider whether your readers understand the point of the comparison. Be sure to remind readers how the comparison works, how the details about the second work you discuss relate to comparable details about the first one discussed. Emphasize similarities between the two by using such words and phrases as "like," "just as," "in the same way," and "another important connection." Emphasize differences with words and phrases such as "Unlike X, Y . . ." or "Although X and Y share . . . they differ in this or that way."

DOING COMPARATIVE ANALYSIS

We would like you to do some comparative analysis by looking at two paintings of family groups. The first is by the American painter Charles Willson Peale (1741–1827); the next, by the French artist Edgar Degas (1834–1917).

We will make a number of observations about the Peale painting and then ask you to make observations about Degas's painting. Before we begin our notes on the Peale family portrait, however, we invite you to look at the painting for about ten minutes and to jot down a list of all the things you notice. At the end of ten minutes, write a few sentences about the painting, conveying your overall reaction to it and your sense of the general impression it conveys.

Comments

Peale's painting reveals a pleasant family, seemingly satisfied with their lives together. The group portrait includes fourteen figures. Nine are immediate living family members, three are busts (most likely of other family members), and one is the family dog. The additional figure is the family nurse, who stands back slightly, indicating perhaps her less intimate relationship to the group.

The family is painted as a tightly knit unit. Some of the family members sit around a table; others lean on and over it. One, a small child, sits on it. And except for the nurse, the members physically touch one another.

Charles Willson Peale, *The Peale Family,* 1773 & 1809. The New York Historical Society.

In noting these details and others, such as the smiling faces, the colors of the clothing, the fruit, the artist at work, we make connections among them and form inferences about the meaning of the painting. We may agree that Peale has portayed a contented and cheerful family united in easy familiarity. The family seems comfortable in its relaxed informality.

But we may notice other things as well. Consider, for example, how the figures are arranged in two groups, six on the left and four on the right. (The dog sits somewhat outside the family circle.) The artist is able to preserve the portrait's unity by means of the table with the child sitting on it. Notice how the left arm of the central figure almost touches the other child's arm and the dress of the woman next to her. Notice also how the fruit fills up the space between the groups, effectively linking them. And notice, too, how the hands of four figures in the larger group are directed toward the smaller group on the right. Finally, consider how the extreme left and right figures look toward each other. Such details unify the family and the composition. This unity is part of the work's meaning as we understand it. It contributes to our sense of the domestic tranquility, the agreeable pleasures of family harmony that Charles Willson Peale depicts.

We now present you, on the following page, with a reproduction of a painting of another family, the Bellelli family, by Edgar Degas.

Edgar Degas, *The Bellelli Family,* 1859. Musée d'Orsay, Paris.

EXERCISES

1. As you look at the Degas painting, make a list of similarities and differences you notice between it and the Peale family portrait. Which seem to predominate, the similarities or the differences? How would you describe the feeling Degas's painting conveys? What leads you to that conclusion?

2. Look carefully at the figures in Degas's painting, especially at their facial expressions and their positions. What do you notice? Based on your observations, what do you infer about the family's relationships? What do you think might be the father's relationship to his daughters? to his wife? What about the relationships between daughters and mother? Based on what you see in Degas' painting, do you think the two girls have the same relationship with their mother? Why or why not?

3. How does Degas's portrayal of the Bellelli family compare with Charles Willson Peale's portrayal of the Peale family?

Comments

Here are a few observations we have made about Degas's painting. Unlike Peale's figures, Degas's are largely separated. Peale's family members smile; Degas's Bellelli's stare blankly. Peale paints with soft warm hues that blend together, whereas Degas employs a sharper, starker set of color contrasts. And although no single figure dominates Peale's canvas, the mother decisively presides over the Bellelli family painting.

Except for the mother and one daughter, the figures seem detached, separated from one another. The greatest visual distance is that between husband and wife. The father sits, while his wife stands. His glance seems directed toward his standing daughter. And he is separated from the other family members by a desk. Moreover, the painter isolates him in still other ways. Unlike the female figures whose faces we see in clearly delineated detail, the father's face is shown only as a vague mass. And instead of being given a frontal or three-quarters view of body and face, as in the depictions of the females, the father is shown seated with part of his back to us.

What are we to make of these observations? How can they lead us toward an interpretation of the painting's significance? Essentially the same way that we made sense of Peale's family portrait: by establishing connections among the details we observe and then drawing inferences from them. We may infer, for example, that the girl who stands close to the mother, whose arm and hand are draped over her daughter's shoulder, is emotionally as well as physically closer to her mother than to her father. We may infer that the other daughter's position between her parents may reflect her attachment to neither—or partly to each, though in uneasy balance. From the abstracted expressions on the faces of the family members, we may infer that they are psychologically detached from one another, each locked in a private world. From the mother's posture, from her placement in the painting, and from her facial expression, we may infer something of her character—something of her severity, perhaps, or her dignity and determination.

Whatever we decide about our understanding of the painting's meaning, one thing seems certain: Degas's Bellellis suggest that family life is not always as cosy, warm, and uncomplicated as Peale's pleasant family portrait suggests. All families are not the same.

EXERCISE

Use the observations you made about both paintings and the author's comments about the paintings to develop your own essay comparing them. Decide whether to use the block method or the alternating approach. Then map out a rough outline for your essay. Finally, write it.

ALTERNATIVE EXERCISE

Find two works of art you would like to compare. Write a paragraph or more comparing them, using the block method. Then rewrite the paragraph using the alternating method.

Guidelines for Comparison

- Compare two things that matter, that seem worth the effort.
- Avoid the apparent or the obvious.
- Compare works that have a significant feature in common, such as genre, style, historical period, subject, situation, or some aspect of technique
- Have a purpose and make a point. Use comparison in the service of an idea, argument, or interpretation.
- Decide which approach to organizing your comparison will be most effective.

A Sample Student Essay

The following essay was written by a first-year student in a humanities course. In her essay, Maile Meloy compares two landscapes by the seventeenth-century Dutch artist Rembrandt van Rijn. Maile sets up her essay primarily in block comparison format, discussing first Rembrandt's *The Three Trees* and following with a discussion of *The Goldweigher's Field.*

Notice how at the end of her introductory paragraph, the writer identifies the areas of interest for her comparison: "certain ideas about nature, civilization, religion, and earthly existence." Notice, too, how in both her introduction and her conclusion, she makes clear both her purpose and her point in developing her comparative analysis.

Maile Meloy

Rembrandt #2

Ben Schmidt

4/5/97

Two Landscapes

With the release of The Netherlands from Spanish control and the development of an oligarchic Dutch nation with a prominent bourgeoisie, came an important turn in the history of art: the birth of Dutch landscape painting. Rembrandt, from the mid-1630s to the mid 1650s, turned his attention to the genre his countrymen virtually invented and for which they established a standard for artists of later years and other nations. The topographical concern for accuracy that is found in the work of other Dutch landscape artists is, however, not found in Rembrandt's work. He is more concerned with conveying the mood and character of the Dutch countryside and the delicacy and drama of nature than in preserving topographical accuracy. His etchings The Three Trees and The Goldweigher's Field demonstrate two very different approaches to the landscape, but both reveal certain ideas about nature, civilization, religion, and earthly existence through a celebration of the newly regained Dutch countryside.

The Three Trees, created in 1643 when Rembrandt was still influenced by the drama of the Baroque tradition, seems particularly symbolic. The storm letting up and the sun breaking through on the Dutch landscape in The Three Trees could be read as the light of new freedom for the Dutch after the storm of Spanish rule, but it can also be reflective of Rembrandt's deeply held religious belief. Rembrandt's dark diagonal slashes at the top left corner of the print are ambiguous in meaning. The slashes seem incongruous with the realism in the rest of the print. Are they rays of divine light breaking through a single hole in the clouds, or sheets of rain moving out of the frame of the picture, clearing the sky? Either way, the expanse of sky and the pervasive quality of the light lend a dramatic quality to the scene, suggestive of the divine in nature.

Ten years later in 1653 Rembrandt would address the biblical image of Christ crucified between the two thieves in The Three Crosses. This later trinity shares more with the first than a similar title; the diagonal slashes that seem almost an afterthought in The Three Trees are added effectively throughout the fourth state of the biblical print to heighten the introspective quality of the scene. Beginnings of this effective use of straight, strong, etched lines over detail can be seen, however, in the earlier work. The trinity image that the prints share gives the landscape a more spiritual mood than it might otherwise have, not being a depiction of a religious subject per se. The protected area underneath the trees, struck by sunlight, suggests the biblical Eden, and an exotic bird leaving the safety of the garden adds to this motif. People as well have left the garden, of course, and they toil and suffer on account of it: peasants plow the field and drive the ox which pulls

The Goldweigher's Field 1651. Etching (12 × 31.9 cm).

the cart, for "cursed is the ground for thy sake. . . . In the sweat of
thy face shall thou eat bread, until thou return to the ground" (Genesis
3). With the loss of paradise, however, came the sexual knowledge that
the lovers share and enjoy in their hidden lower-right corner in the
bushes and the knowledge that allows the draughtsman on the hill to
recreate the day as Rembrandt has done. The exchange was not for naught.

The Goldweigher's Field (1651) has an entirely different theme and
tone. As its title suggests, it is concerned far more with earthly
possession and secular experience than is the earlier print. The
sprawling estate lords over an expanse of land that stretches out to an
almost completely unbroken horizon. The horizon-line divides the print
into two equal halves, giving the earth an importance that the land in
The Three Trees lacks, dominated as it is by the vastness of the sky. The
goldweigher's seemingly boundless property is parcelled and divided and
the trees immediately surrounding the estate are regular and repetitive:
each one is exactly like the next. The broad horizontals of the flat
Dutch countryside are criss-crossed with the energetic diagonals of
roads and tracks. This regularity in the midst of the random
instinctiveness of nature demonstrates humankind's domination over
nature, the bending of the natural to our purposes.

If we assume that the landscape was indeed a commission for the
owner of the field, reasons for certain elements of its composition can
be inferred. The grandeur of the expanse of land and the sense of
ownership and control implicit in the division of the field into

rectangles and roads would appeal to the owner of the estate. The town in the distance is dwarfed in perspective by the vast estate, its town hall a miniature of the goldweigher's country house. The etching is an endorsement of earthly glory and wealth for an individual who has access to such materialistic happiness. Religion is not absent from the scene; the presumably pious burgher has a small church on his estate, recognizable by its steeple, behind the main house to the left. But the focus is not on the divine or on eternal life in exchange for earthly suffering. The focus is on possession and earthly happiness.

The Goldweigher's Field is therefore a more realistic view of the Dutch countryside than the dramatic The Three Trees, in which Rembrandt has romanticized the scene in a manner he typically reserved for paintings. With the inclusion of biblical allusions and the powerful, dominating image of the trees, the etching seems to be more than a faithful recreation of a particular location. This romance is lent by the drama of the sky, in which elusive figures seem to move through the sensual clouds beneath an ominous frame of darkness, and also by a sense of the captured moment, left over from his early years as an artist: the ox and cart are frozen at precisely the moment when the third tree separates the beast from its

The Three Trees. 1643. Etching (21.1 × 28 cm).

burden, the storm is in its crucial stage of lifting, and the lovers are preserved forever in the aesthetic of the almost-kiss.

The characterization of the human figures in <u>The Three Trees</u>, which is absent in <u>The Goldweigher's Field</u>, also lends to its dramatic effect. One of the most brightly lit areas of the print is the figure of the crouched old woman cooking by the river while her husband, almost lost in the shadows, fishes. It is easy to feel like we know their story: they are hungry and cold, but the fishing is good after the rain and the cookfire has not yet gone out on the damp ground. Rembrandt's sensitivity to human figures is evident even in a scene dominated by exaggerated nature. The draughtsman is also emphasized by the whiteness of the paper around him. He sits calmly in the aftermath of the storm, intently studying something out of the frame of the print. In his elevated position and his quiet manner, he seems to possess special knowledge. This fool-on-the-hill figure <u>could be</u> a self-portrait: the introspective Rembrandt who constantly has one eye on himself while knowingly observing the outside world.

The geometric, realistic <u>Goldweigher's Field</u>, while it lacks the drama and detail of the earlier work, is more sensitive in its depiction of the landscape and shows the effectiveness of the late Rembrandt's shorthand style. Where in <u>The Three Trees</u> he is generous with detail and line, here he uses the white of the paper and a spare use of the velvety touch of drypoint to effectively communicate the mood and character of the scene. The Baroque influence of the 1630s is absent and in its place is a less-is-more attitude: a sensitive touch that speaks more eloquently than great detail through its elegant simplicity.

Rembrandt abandoned the genre of landscape soon after the time of <u>The Goldweigher's Field</u>, aware perhaps of what he had achieved with it. From the forbidding density of <u>The Three Trees</u> to the simplicity and the open invitation of the road that rises to meet the viewer in <u>The Goldweigher's Field</u> is a remarkable transition, one that echoes his progression in other genres. Each reflects the period of Rembrandt's artistic life in which it was painted, and each conveys an idea and a mood through the depiction of the land and its inhabitants. Where they differ in style and in the message they convey, they share the communicative power for which Rembrandt is lauded.

4
Writing from Different Critical Perspectives

In writing about works of visual and verbal art, critics (and students) invariably write from one or another critical perspective, sometimes without being aware of that fact. In some cases, writers explicitly announce their critical approach; in other instances, they leave their critical approach unstated and implicit.

It is important to recognize that all analysis and interpretation of artworks is grounded in some type of critical approach or interpretive perspective. Being aware of the assumptions of various critical perspectives enables us to recognize their limitations and their uses. For example, the kinds of assumptions that govern a historically minded critical approach alert us to how historical conditions such as patronage or patriarchal power affect the creation and dissemination of works of art, music, and literature. From attending to the approach that historical critics take to artworks, we can see things in and about those works that we might overlook without their historical critical perspective.

And yet, even as we become aware of the advantages of a historical critical perspective, we need to be aware of what this approach leaves out—in short, its limitations. Historical critics may ignore other artistic elements and other values of works of art, such as their use of line and color, their control of language, their control of form, their shaping of artistic materials, whether these be the materials of sculpture or architecture, of painting or poetry, of music or theater or film.

The point, simply, is that different critical perspectives yield different kinds of understanding about works of art because they emphasize different aspects of their creation, production, and dissemination. Because all critical perspectives are inherently limited, it is useful to be familiar with a range of critical approaches to analyzing and interpeting the arts of various cultures. You will find that familiarity with a range of critical perspectives will help you write more engaging, interesting, and persuasive papers and reports about arts and culture.

This chapter identifies some of the more common and important critical perspectives employed in the humanities today. These include the following critical approaches: formalist, historical, biographical, psychological, sociocultural, and mythological. For each of these critical perspectives you will find an overview that explains its main features and a set of questions you can use to apply each critical perspective to another work of art, literature, or music.

FORMALIST PERSPECTIVES

Formalist critics emphasize the form of a work of art to determine its meaning, focusing on literary elements such as plot, character, setting, diction, imagery, structure, and point of view; on artistic elements such as line, color, volume, materials, scale, and perspective; and on musical elements such as melody, harmony, rhythm, dynamics, and form. Approaching works of art as independent systems with interdependent parts, formalists typically subordinate biographical information or historical data in their interpretations. Underlying a formalist critical perspective is the belief that works of literature and music, like paintings and sculptures, are unified artistic wholes that can be understood by analyzing their parts.

According to the formalist view, the proper concern of criticism is with the work itself rather than with literary, artistic, or musical history; the life and mind of the author; or a work's social and cultural contexts. For a formalist, the central meaning of a literary work is discovered through a detailed analysis of the work's formal elements rather than by going outside the work to consider other issues, whether biographical, historical, psychological, social, political, or ideological. Such additional considerations, from the formalist perspective, are extrinsic, or external, and of secondary importance. What matters most to the formalist critic is how the work comes to mean what it does—how its resources of language are deployed by the writer, artist, or composer to convey meaning. Implicit in the formalist perspective, moreover, is that readers, viewers, and listeners can indeed determine the meanings of works of art, such as poems and paintings, novels and symphonies. And further implicit in this perspective is that the greatest artworks are "universal," their wholeness and aesthetic harmony transcending the specific particularities they describe.

The primary method of formalism is a close reading of the work of art, with an emphasis, for example, on a literary work's use of metaphor or symbol, its deployment of irony, its patterns of image or action. Poetry lends itself especially well to the kinds of close reading favored by formalist critics because its language tends to be more compressed and metaphorical than prose—at least as a general rule. Nonetheless, formal analysis of novels and plays can also focus on close reading of key passages (the opening and closing chapters of a novel, for example; or the first and last scenes of a play; or a climactic moment in the action of drama, poetry, or fiction). In addition, formalist critics analyze the large-scale structures of longer works, looking for patterns and relationships among scenes, actions, and characters. Formalist critics of music, painting, and sculpture employ similar categories of analysis, with formalist art critics, for example, focusing on a work's use of line and color, its balances and harmonies of shape and volume, and its overall relationship of parts and elements in an integrated aesthetic whole.

One of the consistent features of formalist criticism is an emphasis on tension and ambiguity. Tension refers to the way elements of a work reflect conflict and opposition. Ambiguity refers to the ways artworks remain open to more than a single, unified, definite interpretation. Both tension and ambiguity as elements of formalist critical approaches were picked up and elaborated to serve different interpretive arguments by critics who employ the critical methods known as structuralism and deconstruction.

Formalist Critical Questions

1. How is the work organized? How does it begin? How is it shaped, developed, or structured?

2. What is the relationship of each part of the work to the work as a whole? How are the parts related to one another?

For Literary Works:

1. Who is narrating or telling what happens in the work? How is the narrator, speaker, or character revealed to readers? How do we come to know and understand the figure?

2. Who are the major and minor characters? What do they represent? How do they relate to one another?

3. What are the time and place of the work—its setting? How is the setting related to what we know of the characters and their actions? To what extent is the setting symbolic?

4. What kind of language does the author use to describe, narrate, explain, or otherwise create the world of the literary work? More specifically, what images, similes, metaphors, and symbols appear in the work? What is their funtion? What meanings do they convey?

HISTORICAL PERSPECTIVES

Historical critics approach works of art in two ways: (1) they provide a context of background information necessary for understanding how artworks were perceived in their time and (2) they show how works of art reflect ideas and attitudes of the time in which they were created. These two general approaches to historical criticism represent methods that might be termed "old historicism" and "new historicism," respectively.

The older form of historical criticism, still in use today, insists that a work of art be approached with a sense of its historical context. This is necessary, insist such historical critics, because every artwork is a product of its world and time. Understanding the social background and the intellectual currents of that world and time illuminate works of art for later generations.

Knowing something about the London of William Blake's time, for example, helps readers better appreciate and understand the power of Blake's protest against horrific social conditions and the institutions of church and state which Blake held responsible for permitting such conditions to exist. In his poem "London," Blake refers to chimney sweepers, who were usually young children small enough to fit inside a chimney, whose parents sent them to a kind of work that drastically curtailed their childhood and their lives.

Like earlier historical approaches, a more contemporary approach identified as "new historicism" considers historical contexts of works of art essential for understanding and appreciating them. A significant difference, however, is that new historicism emphasizes analyzing historical documents with the same intensity as the artworks being interpreted.

An important feature of new historicist criticism is its concern with examining the power relations of rulers and subjects. A guiding assumption among many new historicist critics is that not only works of art but also documents, records, even institutions such as hospitals and prisons, are ideological products culturally constructed from the prevailing power structures that dominate particular societies. Interpreting a work of art from a new historicist perspective thus becomes an exercise in uncovering the conflicting and subversive perspectives of the marginalized and suppressed.

While appropriating some of the methods of formalist critics, new historicists differ from them in important ways. Unlike critics who limit their analysis of a work of art to its literary or artistic elements, new historicists analyze the cultural context embedded in the artwork and explain its relationship with the network of assumptions and beliefs that inform cultural practices prevalent in the time the work was created. Moreover, new historicist critics do not see history as mere "background" against which to study works of art, but rather view history as an equally important "text," one that is ultimately inseparable from works of art, which inevitably reveal the conflicting power relations that underlie human social interaction.

New Historicist Critical Questions

1. When was the artwork created? How was it received by its audience?

2. What does the work's reception reveal about the standards of taste and value during the period when it was produced and disseminated?

3. What social attitudes and cultural practices related to the work were prevalent during the time of its composition?

4. How were power relations reflected in the work manifested in the social institutions prevalent during the time of its production and reception?

5. What other types of historical documents, cultural artifacts, or social institutions might be analyzed in conjunction with particular works of art? How might such an analysis illuminate those particular artworks?

BIOGRAPHICAL PERSPECTIVES

To what extent the life of a writer, artist, or composer should be brought to bear on an interpretation of his or her work has long been a matter of controversy. Some critics insist that biographical information at best distracts from and at worst distorts the process of analyzing and interpreting works of art. These critics believe that works of art must stand on their own, stripped of their relationship to the artists' lives.

Against this view, however, biographical critics argue that three kinds of benefits result from using artists' lives in interpreting their works: (1) facts about artists' experiences help readers, viewers, and listeners interpret their works more accurately; (2) an understanding of an artist's life makes his or her audience more appreciative of the artist's difficulties in creating works of art; and (3) the audience for an artist's, writer's, or composer's work can better asssess the creator's preoccupations by studying how they modify, adapt, and transform their experience in works of art.

Knowing, for example, that Shakespeare and Molière were actors who performed in the plays they wrote provides an added dimension to our appreciation of their creative genius. Moreover, it might also invite us to look at their plays from the practical standpoint of a performer rather than only from the perspective of a reader, student, or theatergoer. Or knowing that Beethoven became deaf during the most creative period of his life or that Mozart, after a period of being celebrated and courted by royalty, died a pauper not only enhances our appreciation of these composers' struggles, but also inspires us to listen in new ways to their music. Or knowing that the Mexican painter Frida Kahlo suffered severe injury in an automobile accident as a teenager and later married the prominent artist Diego Rivera, who was repeatedly unfaithful to her, helps us appreciate the ways Kahlo draws our attention to the theme of suffering in her art, particularly in her many self-portraits.

Biographical Critical Questions

1. What events or experiences in the artist's, writer's, or composer's life does the work reflect?

2. In what ways and to what extent does the artist's experience affect the artist's works?

PSYCHOLOGICAL PERSPECTIVES

Psychological critics approach a work of art as the revelation of its creator's mind and personality. They view artworks as intimately linked with their creators' mental and emotional characteristics. Like biographical critics, psychological critics use what they know of writers', artists', and composers' lives to explain features of their work.

Some psychological critics are more interested in the creative process than in the artworks produced; these critics look to artworks as clues to the creative imagination. Other psychological critics focus on artists' behavior and its motivations. Still others employ methods of Freudian psychoanalysis to understand not just the works artists create but also, in the case of literature, the characters writers create, such as Shakespeare's Hamlet or Sophocles' Oedipus.

Psychoanalytic criticism derives from Freud's revolutionary psychology, in which he developed the notion of the unconscious, along with the psychological mechanisms of displacement, fixation, and manifest and latent dream content (among others). Freud posited an unconscious element of the mind below the subconscious, which exists just beneath the threshhold of conscious awareness. According to Freud, the unconscious harbors forbidden wishes and desires, often sexual, which conflict with an individual's or society's moral standards. Freud explains, that although the individual represses or "censors" these unconscious fantasies and desires, they become "displaced" or distorted in dreams and fantasies, which serve to disguise their real meaning. The disguised versions that appear in a person's conscious life are considered to be the "manifest" representations of the unconscious wishes that are their "latent" content, which psychoanalytic critics attempt to discover and explain. Psychoanalytic critics rely heavily on symbolism to identify and explain the meaning of repressed desires, by interpreting ordinary objects such as clocks and towers as well as natural elements such as fire and water in ways that reveal aspects of human sexuality.

Among the most important of the categories derived from Freud that psychoanalytic critics employ are those that Freud used to describe mental structures and dynamics. Freud recognized three types of mental functions, which he designated the id, the ego, and the superego. Freud saw the id as the storehouse of desires, primarily libidinal or sexual, but also aggressive and possessive. He saw the superego as the representative of societal and parental standards of ethics and morality. And he saw the ego as the negotiator between the desires and demands of the id and the controlling and constraining force of the superego, all influenced further by an individual's relationship with other people in the contexts of actual life. These few but important psychoanalytic concepts have been put to varied uses by critics using a range of psychological approaches. Freud himself analyzed Sophocles' tragic drama *Oedipus the King* to explain how Oedipus harbored an unconscious desire to kill his father and marry his mother, events the play accounts for. Other critics have used Freud's insights to analyze the hidden motivations of literary characters. Hamlet, for example, has stimulated psychological critics of all persuasions to explain why he delays King Claudius, who murdered Hamlet's father and married Queen Gertrude, Hamlet's mother.

Psychological Critical Questions

1. What connections can you make between your knowledge of an author's, artist's, or composer's life and the behavior and motivations of characters, figures, or motifs in his or her work?

2. How does your understanding of the characters, figures, or motifs in an artist's work help you understand his or her mental world and imaginative life?

For Literature

3. To what extent can you employ the concepts of Freudian psychoanalysis to explain the motivations of literary characters?

SOCIOCULTURAL PERSPECTIVES

Like historical and biographical critics, sociocultural critics argue that artworks should not be isolated from the social and cultural contexts in which they have been created. And like historical critics of the new historicist persuasion, sociocultural critics emphasize how power relations are played out in society. Sociocultural critics focus on societal values and how those values are reflected and embedded. At one end of the sociocultural critical spectrum, works of art are treated simply as documents that either embody social conditions or are a product of those conditions. Critics employing a sociocultural perspective study the economic, political, social, and cultural issues expressed in works of art.

Two significant trends in sociocultural criticism have had a decisive impact on critical approaches to the arts: Marxist criticism and feminist criticism. Proponents of each of these critical perspectives have used some of the tools of other critical approaches, such as the close readings of the formalists and the symbolic analysis of psychoanalytic critics, to espouse their respective ideologies in interpreting works of art.

Marxist Perspectives

Marxist critics, who are indebted to the political theory of Karl Marx and Friedrich Engels, examine literature for its reflection of how dominant elite and middle-class bourgeois values lead to the control and suppression of the working class. Marxist critics see literature's value in promoting social and economic revolution, with works that espouse Marxist ideology serving to prompt the kinds of economic and political changes that conform to Marxist principles. Such changes would include the overthrow of the dominant bourgeois capitalist ideology and the loss of power by those with money, land, and privilege. Marxist criticism is concerned both with understanding the role of politics, money, and power in works of art and with redefining and reforming the way society distributes its resources among the classes. Fundamentally, the Marxist ideology looks toward a vision of a world where class conflict has disappeared along with social classes.

A sociocultural approach to the study of Chekhov's *Cherry Orchard,* for example, might focus on the changing conditions society was undergoing in Russia at the end of the nineteenth century. Of particular importance would be the passing of an aristocratic way of life represented by the Ranevskaya family and its replacement by a new type of entrepreneurship seen in Yermolay Lopahin, a merchant, who buys the Ranevskaya's beloved cherry orchard with the intention of cutting it down and building houses on the property. The shift of power and money from one social class, the landed aristocracy, to another, a middle class rising to replace it, would become a central locus of interest for the sociocultural critic of Chekhov's play. Other of the play's themes, such as the characters' lack of fulfillment, their lost chances for love and happiness, and the lack of understanding and communication in the characters' relationships, would be less important than what the play reveals about social, economic, and cultural conditions at work in society at the time.

Marxist Critical Questions

1. What social, cultural, and economic forces and institutions are represented in the work? How are these forces portrayed?

2. What political elements, if any, appear in the work? How important are they?

3. To what extent are the characters or figures depicted in the work affected by social, cultural, political, or economic forces?

Feminist Perspectives

Feminist criticism, like Marxist and new historicist criticism, examines the social and cultural aspects of artworks, especially for what those works reveal about the role, position, and influence of women. Like other socially and culturally minded critics, feminist critics consider works of art in relation to their social and cultural contexts and content.

Feminist critics see works of art as an arena to contest for power and control, and, like other sociocultural critics, as agents for social transformation. Moreover, feminist critics seek to redress the imbalance of attention and value traditionally accorded male artists, writers, and characters by attending to works by and about women. Feminist critics have looked, for example, at how feminine consciousness has been portrayed in literature. They have investigated why so few women composed symphonies and have discovered previously neglected composers as well as novelists, poets, and painters.

Feminist criticism has also uncovered patriarchal and masculinist assumptions about the production and reception of works of art. They have shown how often typical or normal experience represented in works of art has been assumed to be male and how female sensibilities and perspectives have been marginalized when not entirely neglected. Feminist critics have made a concerted effort to examine works of the traditional canon of literature and art, especially through "the prism of gender," changing not only the questions asked about works of art, but also what is discovered about them through asking questions about gender.

Feminist Critical Questions

1. To what extent does the representation of women (and men) in the work reflect the place and time in which the work was written?

2. To what extent does the representation of women (and men) in the work conflict with the historical circumstances of the work's composition?

3. How are the relations between men and women presented in the work? What roles do men and women assume and perform, and with what consequences?

MYTHOLOGICAL PERSPECTIVES

In general terms, a "myth" is a story that explains how something came to be. Every culture creates stories to explain what it considers important, valuable, and true. Thus the Greek myth of Persephone, who was kidnapped by Pluto, the god of the underworld, and allowed to return to her mother, Demeter, every year explains the changes of the seasons. Or the biblical story of Eve's temptation by the serpent in the book of Genesis, which concludes with God's curse of the serpent, explains, among other things, why snakes crawl.

Myth criticism, however, is not as concerned with stories that explain origins as much as with those that provide universal story patterns that recur with regularity among many cultures and in many different times and places. The story patterns that myth critics typically identify and analyze are those that represent common, familiar, even universal human experiences, such as being born and dying, growing up and crossing the threshold into adulthood, going on a journey, engaging in sexual activity. These familiar patterns of human action and experience, however, are of interest to myth critics not primarily in and of themselves, but rather for how they represent religious beliefs, social customs, and cultural attitudes.

Birth, for example, is of interest as a symbolic beginning, and death, as a symbolic ending. A journey is a symbolic venturing out into the world to explore and experience what it has in store for the traveler. Sleeping and dreaming are not simply states of ordinary experience, but symbolic modes of entrance to another realm and an envisioning of unusual and perhaps strange possibilities unimagined in waking life. So, too, with physical contests, sexual encounters, and other forms of experience, which many times are occasions for individuals to be tested, challenged, and perhaps initiated into an advanced or superior state of being—becoming a warrior, for example, or a mother, a prophet, or a king.

Myth critics discover in artworks of all times and places stories with basic patterns that can be explained in terms of **archetypes,** or universal symbols. Some mythological critics believe that archetypes are part of every person's unconscious mind, a kind of collective unconscious that each of us inherits by virtue of our common humanity. Besides the fundamental facts of human existence, other archetypes include typical literary characters such as the Don Juan or womanizer, the femme fatale or dangerous female, the trickster or con artist, the damsel in distress, the rebel, the tyrant, the hero, the betrayer. Creatures real and imaginary can also be archetypal symbols. The lion, for example, represents strength; the eagle, independence; the fox, cunning; the unicorn, innocence; the dragon, destruction; the centaur, the union of matter and spirit, animality and humanity, or even humanity and divinity.

It is on plot or the sequence of causally related incidents and actions, however, that myth criticism focuses most heavily. The archetypal images, creatures, and characters exist within stories that themselves exhibit patterns of recurrence. So, for example, there are stories of the arduous quest fraught with perils through which a protagonist must survive, perhaps to rescue an innocent victim, perhaps to prove his superior courage or morality, perhaps to save others from destruction. There are stories of vengeance, of death and rebirth, of resurrection, of transformation from one kind or stage of being into another, stories of enlightenment, of devastation, of lost paradises. Many such stories can be found in the religious literature of cultures around the world. The Bible, for example, contains stories of creation

(Adam and Eve), fraternal rivalry and murder (Cain and Abel), destruction (Noah) and forgiveness (the Ark and the Covenant), wandering and enslavement (the Exodus), death and resurrection (Jesus' life and ministry)— and so on. This list can be multiplied by consulting, for example, the Taoist and Confucian religious traditions of China, the Hindu traditions of India and the Buddhist traditions of Japan, or the Islamic tradition, to make only the smallest of starts.

What a mythological critic does with archetypal characters, stories, creatures, and even natural elements such as sun and moon, darkness and light, fire and water, is to link them up with one another, to see one literary work in relation to others of a similar type. Thus, for example, Hamlet's revenge of his father's death can be linked with myths from other cultures that include a son's avenging his father. Or the story of Hamlet can be linked with others in which the corruption poisoning a country has been eliminated through some action taken by the hero.

Mythological Critical Questions

1. What incidents in the work seem common or familiar enough as actions that they might be considered symbolic or archetypal? Are there any journeys, battles, falls, reversals of fortune?

2. What kinds of character types appear in the work? How might they be classified?

3. What creatures, elements of nature, or human-made objects play a role in the work? To what extent might they be considered symbolic?

4. What changes do the characters undergo? How can those changes be characterized or named? To what might they be related or compared?

5. What religious or quasireligious traditions with which you are familiar might the work's story, characters, elements, or objects be compared to or affiliated with?

SELECTING AND USING CRITICAL PERSPECTIVES

One of your more difficult decisions regarding using critical perspectives will be choosing those that are especially appropriate and effective for analyzing a particular work of art. Not every critical perspective will yield fruitful results applied to every work of art. Some critical perspectives will make a better fit than others for particular works. In addition, you can combine critical perspectives, bringing more than one to bear in analyzing a work of art.

A danger in using any critical approach is that the work of art may be distorted in an attempt to make it fit a particular critical perspective. Some critics apply their favorite critical perspective mechanically with little regard for the integrity of the artworks analyzed. Some put every work through the same ideological meatgrinder, with every work ground into the same kind of critical hamburger.

One way to avoid this danger is to consider the various critical approaches as interpretive possibilities rather than as formulas for producing an interpretation. Try to experience the intellectual playfulness and imaginative resourcefulness possible in applying various critical perspectives to works of art.

When you write about a work of art, consider the various critical perspectives as ways into the work, as ways to illumine its different parts, aspects, and contexts. You can use the questions that accompany each critical perspective to prompt freewriting, annotating, and questioning which should lead you to insights about the works you write about. Use the critical questions to stimulate your thinking; then, see which critical perspectives yield the best results for thinking and writing.

WRITING ABOUT

THE
HUMANITIES

5
Writing About Art
and Music

In addition to the general principles of interpreting and writing about the humanities discussed in previous chapters, we must now attend in more detail to some particular aspects of writing about particular disciplines. This chapter will focus on writing about art and music; the following chapter will consider writing about works of literature.

WRITING ABOUT ART

Why write about works of art? We write about artworks in part because writing about them helps us to better understand and appreciate them. Writing forces us to concentrate on seeing what is before our eyes so that we will have something to say. Writing about a work of art encourages us to slow down and observe more carefully than we might do otherwise. And writing about a work of art allows us to express our feelings and develop our thinking about what the work says to us, why it says what it does, and perhaps how it conveys it as well.

Painting

Before writing about a painting, you need to look carefully at it (or a reproduction of the work). In doing so, you will be making observations about the following elements: genre, medium, composition, perspective,

64

texture, contour or shape, line, space, color, light. Let's take these up briefly, one at a time.

By genre we mean the type or category of painting a particular work belongs to—a portrait, for example, a still life, or a landscape. Some paintings contain elements of two or more genres, as for example, Leonardo da Vinci's famous *Mona Lisa,* which, though primarily a portrait, also contains a background landscape. In viewing a painting, begin by focusing on its most immediate generic elements—on what seems most important. If there is action, identify what is happening. If there are multiple figures, consider their relation to one another. If still life objects are portrayed along with figures, consider the relationship of figures to objects, and so on.

In Chapter 3, you looked at group portraits of the Peale and Bellelli families. In Chapter 1, you looked at a portrait of Vincent van Gogh, along with his *Starry Night.* The kinds of questions that guided your examination of reproductions of those paintings were specific to those works. In this chapter, we will provide some broader questions you can use when viewing paintings in different genres.

When looking at a portrait, for example, you should consider the extent to which the portrait emphasizes surface features of the sitter—his or her clothing, for example—or whether it somehow probes beneath to reveal something of the figure's personality or character. This is not an easy matter, however, as viewers interpret details of facial expression, body posture, and gesture differently.

Use the following questions to help yourself slow down and absorb portraits:*

- How much of the figure does the artist portray?
- What do the figure's clothing and accessories contribute to our understanding of the picture's period and its social world?
- What does the angle at which the figure is presented suggest about the figure's attitude? How do the figure's facial expression and bodily posture convey his or her personality?
- Does the picture seem to emphasize the individuality of the figure (perhaps by presenting him or her against a dark background and with minimal attention to details of dress and accessories)? Or does the picture seem to emphasize the social or political importance of the figure (perhaps by accentuating accessories and details of dress)?

---

*For the questions about painting and for those on sculpture, architecture, and photography, I am indebted to the fifth edition of Sylvan Barnet's *Writing About Art.*

- Is the figure presented still or in motion? from the front, in profile, in three-quarters view?
- In portraits of two or more figures, do the figures look at or touch each other? What is suggested by their contact or lack of it?

You may wish to look back to the self-portrait of van Gogh in Chapter 1 and the family portraits of Peale and Degas in Chapter 3.

Landscapes, too, can be approached with some common questions in mind. If the landscape does not contain human figures, focus on the artist's rendering of the natural scene. Consider the kind of scene depicted and what the artist seems to emphasize in its rendering. Is a storm depicted, for example, or a broad vista? What image of nature is suggested in the work?

Here are some additional questions to ask yourself when viewing landscapes:

- What does the landscape suggest about the natural world?
- What relationship exists between nature and the human figures depicted? In looking at van Gogh's *Starry Night,* for example, you notice that the stars and sky occupy about three-quarters of the canvas, with the village much smaller in scale.
- Can the landscape be interpreted symbolically? How might it be read from a psychological, spiritual, economic, or political perspective?
- What social implications might the landscape bear?
- To what extent might its origin or cultural context help us interpret it? Chinese landscape paintings sometimes bear inscriptions that comment directly or indirectly on the work's significance.

In viewing any work of art, you should also pay attention to its title, which often provides information about genre, historical and other contexts, and the medium in which it was created, such as fresco or oil. A work's medium represents a conscious choice on the part of the artist and, as such, merits attention. Here are some questions to consider about medium:

- If a painting, is it painted in oil, in tempera (pigment dissolved in egg), in gesso? Is the paint layed on in thin layers, or thickly and heavily (impasto)?
- Is the painting done on canvas? on paper? on wood? on silk? With what effects?
- If a drawing, was it done on paper with a high or low degree of absorbency? with a wet medium, such as ink applied with a pen, or a dry medium, such as chalk or pencil?

Thomas Cole, *American Lake Scene,* 1844, oil on canvas, 18¼ × 24½″ (46.4 × 62.2 cm). Detroit Institute of Arts.

Frederic Edwin Church, American, 1826–1900. *Twilight in the Wilderness,* 1860, oil on canvas, 3′4″ × 5′4″ (101.6 × 162.6 cm). Cleveland Museum of Art.

An artist's choice of medium affects the qualities of color in a painting. The intensity or brightness of a color is referred to as its "value"; that is, its relative lightness or darkness of hue. *Hue* refers to the name of a color: blue or red, for example. Hues that are vivid are said to be of high saturation and, correspondingly, pale hues are described as being of low saturation.

Be careful about making too large claims for color in a painting, as a work's colors may have changed over time—as the restoration of Michelangelo's painting of the Sistine Chapel ceiling has recently shown. (Over the centuries, the colors of the ceiling had darkened to a sombre value. When cleaned, the painting's colors were revealed to be far brighter than most viewers of the ceiling had ever imagined.) Remember, too, that the colors of objects in a painting may appear darker or lighter, brighter or less intense, in relation to other objects and colors included in the painting.

The color of a painting is related to the effects of light produced in it. Try to identify the light source in the paintings you view. Where does the light seem to come from? Is the light bright or muted? Does it produce sharply defined contrasts in the painting, or not? Are some areas of the painting—a particular figure, or a part of a figure such as a face, highlighted? If so, to what effect?

Besides color and light, a number of other considerations can be addressed when you look at paintings. Here are a few more questions you can use to enhance your ability to see aspects of paintings so you will have more to say about them when you write:

- What is the focus of the composition? What is emphasized?
- Is the composition balanced? symmetrical? harmonious? With what effects?
- Does the work emphasize diagonal or vertical lines, which suggest motion and energy? Or is it mostly horizontal, which suggests tranquillity? (Look back at van Gogh's *Starry Night* to see the thrusting vertical made by the cypress tree.)
- Does the work convey a sense of depth or recession in space, or do the figures and objects appear lined up in a flat plane?
- What is the shape and size of the work? (Be aware that, when looking at reproductions in books and at slides, a work's size may be distorted. A tiny painting and a giant canvas pictured on a half-page spread look similar in size, when in reality, they differ dramatically.
- What is the scale, or relative size, of objects and figures in relation to the size of the canvas or other medium on which they are painted?

Photography

We are so familiar with photographs that it may be difficult to think of them as works of art. And, in fact, many photographs are literally snapshots taken without conscious artistic intent. Nonetheless, it is worth looking closely at the kinds of photographs that have been taken with thought and care—with a concern for what the photograph expresses as well as for its ostensible surface image.

It is important to realize that what a photographer sees when taking a photograph is more than and often quite different from the resulting photographic image. In other words, any photograph is a selection from a wealth of details that the photograph did not include in the finished picture. Moreover, photographers often doctor their photographs, cropping and otherwise altering the image as it was originally photographed by the camera.

Without going into the intricacies of the photographic process, we can see that photographers control and select, arrange and shape the images they finally put forth, just as painters do with their finished canvases. Here are a few questions to guide your consideration of photographs. You can also use some of the questions associated with paintings.

- What does the photograph depict? That is, what is its subject?
- What is the relationship among the figures depicted?
- Is it in color or black and white? How does the color or lack of color fit the subject of the photograph?
- Who took the photograph, under what conditions, and for what purpose? Was it an individual or a group project?
- What is its title, and was the title provided by the photographer, or was it added later? Under what circumstances?
- What are the photograph's dimensions? Has it been trimmed or cropped or otherwise altered? With what effects?
- What details are visible? What is focused on most sharply? Is any part of the photograph left fuzzy or in soft focus? With what effects?
- What kind of lighting does the photograph suggest or exhibit? Under what lighting conditions was it taken—indoors or out? What effect is created by the lighting?
- What process was used to develop the photograph?
- What does the photograph "say" or suggest?

Henri Cartier-Bresson, *Gare St. Lazare, Paris,* 1932.

Dmitri Baltermants, *Attack!,* 1941.

Sculpture

For sculptures that are portraits, some of the questions listed earlier for paintings can be applied. Consider in particular whether the sculpture represents an individual or a type; that is, whether your sense is more of a particular person or of a category or a symbol—of a ruler or a deity, for example. Paradoxically, you may find that an image that seems highly specified and individualistic is simultaneously more broadly representative or symbolic.

Other kinds of questions to ask yourself about works of sculpture are these:

- Why was the sculpture made? What purpose was it designed to serve? How or what does it represent?
- What kind of pose does it hold? Rodin's *Thinker* sits very differently from the sitting pose of Abraham Lincoln in the Lincoln Memorial. What is implied or conveyed by the figure's pose?
- Is the figure draped or nude? Michelangelo's nude *David* can be contrasted with Bernini's draped *David* (see page 72). What does the drapery reveal about the body beneath it? What does it conceal? To what extent does the drapery accentuate motion or a pattern echoed by the figure or its larger context (as, for example, its placement on a throne or in a wall niche)?
- What material is the sculpture made of—clay, wood, granite, marble? Is its surface smooth or rough? What does the medium and texture "say" about the figure represented?
- To what extent is the figure carved, and to what extent is it modeled or shaped? How does its surface absorb, hold, reflect light and shadow? To what effect?
- Is the subject depicted in motion or still? What does its silhouette suggest?
- Is the figure now, or was it once, painted? With what colors and to what effect? What does the color of its paint or its material contribute to the impression that the figure makes?
- How big is the sculpture? Michelangelo's *David* is larger than life, whereas Bernini's is life size. What is the effect of the difference?
- What was the original site of the sculpture? Has it been removed from that site? If so, what is the difference between viewing it at the original site and in a museum? Is the sculpture mounted on a base? To what extent is the base part of the sculpture?
- What is the best position from which to view it?

Left: Michelangelo, *David,* 1501–04, marble, height 13′5″ (4.09 m). Galleria dell'Accademia, Florence. *Right:* Gianlorenzo Bernini, *David,* 1623, marble, height 5′7″ (1.7 m). Galleria Borghese, Rome.

Architecture

Like paintings, sculptures, and works of literature, works of architecture can be viewed in relation to their time and place of construction. In fact, works of architecture, because they are made for a practical purpose, must be considered in relation to the societies reponsible for producing them. The question is less academic than practical.

A work of architecture, such as a church or a public building, can be considered from the standpoint of its purpose or function—why it was made; its structural soundness—how well it is made; and its design—how beautifully it has been made. We take up these three essential architectural aspects briefly, one at a time.

First, purpose. Was the work constructed for a single specific purpose, as for example a Buddhist temple or a Gothic cathedral for worship? Has the original purpose of the building been supplanted by another at a later period, as for example converting a ruler's palace into a legislative assembly or a museum? Has the building been expanded, contracted, remodeled, renovated, restored, or in any way altered? If so, with what results?

How does the building fit into its surrounding context—its neighborhood, its building site? Is it integrated into its surroundings, or does it stand out from them? Was this the original intention of the architect? To what extent have its surroundings changed? How well is it related to other buildings and structures that have been erected since it was constructed?

Second, structure. How solidly is it built? Has it held up over time? Is it structurally sound? To what extent do its interior spaces fit the purposes for which they were originally designed? That is, to what extent does form follow function? To what extent might the form be symbolic—representing tranquillity or energy, for example?

Of what materials is it made? What associations do its materials have—marble and granite suggest power and prestige, durability and dignity. Wood is humbler but can suggest simplicity and rusticity if left "natural," and if smoothly sanded and painted, something more communal, perhaps more "finished."

Third, design. It perhaps seems strange to ask what a building suggests or expresses in the way we might consider a sculpture or a painting expressive. Nonetheless, a building's size and scale, its shape and form, color and texture, speak to the same kinds of aesthetic issues and responses that works of art do. What does a structure's design contribute to its "meaning"?

And, more specifically, you can ask other kinds of questions about architectural structures:

- Is it ornamented or decorated in any way, and if so, how, and to what effect? How are its interior spaces arranged, divided, allocated?
- What are its walls and floors made of—brick? wood? marble? To what effect?
- What colors are its walls and floors and ceilings?
- Does the building seem warm and inviting? Or does it seem cold and forbidding?
- How is it lighted? What place does natural daylight have in its design? What aesthetic effect does light—both natural and artificial—have on the overall feeling the building creates?
- To what extent does the building represent either a particular individual's architectural philosophy or a sociocultural architectural style or perspective.

WRITING ABOUT MUSIC

Among those who have written about music clearly and engagingly are the Irish playwright and critic George Bernard Shaw, the American composer Aaron Copland, the jazz critic Whitney Balliett, and the contemporary American composer, conductor, and teacher Leonard Bernstein.

Here, for example, is Leonard Bernstein describing a theme in the work of the Russian composer Peter Ilych Tchaikovsky:

> Let's just see how Tchaikovsky went about building up that lovely theme of his by simply repeating his ideas in a certain arranged order—what I like to call the 1-2-3 method. In fact so many famous themes are formed by exactly this method that I think you ought to know about it. Here's how it works: first of all there is a short idea, or phrase: (musical quote)— second, the same phrase is repeated, but with a small variation: (musical quote)—and third, the tune takes off in a flight of inspiration: (musical quote). 1, 2, and 3—like a 3-stage rocket, or like the countdown in a race: "On your mark, get set, go!" Or in target practice: "Ready, aim, fire!" Or in a movie studio: "Lights, camera, action!" It's always the same 1, 2, and 3!

Bernstein uses a series of similes, comparisons using "like," to explain how Tchaikovsky's theme contains three parts. The comparisons he makes are with things familiar to his audience—a group of children attending a lecture and concert.

Here is another example of a writer, this time the composer Aaron Copland, describing the musical element of timbre:

> After rhythm, melody, and harmony, comes timbre, or tone color. Just as it is impossible to hear speech without hearing some specific timbre, so music can exist only in terms of some specific color in tone. Timbre in music is analogous to color in painting . . . Just as most mortals know the difference between white and green, so the recognition of differences in tone color is an innate sense with which most of us are born. It is difficult to imagine a person so "tone-blind" that he cannot tell a bass voice from a soprano, or, to put it instrumentally, a tuba from a cello.

Like Bernstein, Copland makes a comparison with something his audience understands, to help them understand something unfamiliar to them. Where Bernstein used simile, Copland develops an analogy, or extended comparison.

In addition to writing about music directly as do Bernstein and Copland, you can also write around the music, talking about music without actually describing what it sounds like. You might write about the life and times of a composer or performer; you might write about the reasons for the rise and decline in popularity of a particular instrument or musical form or style; you might write about a composer's or performer's influence, such as that of Beethoven or the Beatles. You could write a review of a record or of a concert. You could raise and answer questions such as "Why do people listen to music?" or "What is the future of rap (or of rock)?" You could write an analysis of a popular song, accounting for the effectiveness of its lyrics and for the way its music—melody, rhythm, and so on— supports its words. In short, there are many ways to write productively about music without having to worry about getting overly technical about it.

Here, for example, is the American writer Ralph Ellison writing about the gospel singer Mahalia Jackson:

> There are certain women singers who possess, beyond all the boundaries of our admiration for their art, an uncanny power to evoke our love. We warm with pleasure at mere mention of their names; their simplest songs sing in our hearts like the remembered voices of old dear friends, and when we are lost within the listening anonymity of darkened concert halls, they seem to seek us out unerringly. Standing regal within the bright isolation of the stage, their subtlest effects seem meant for us and us alone; privately, as across the intimate space of our own living rooms. And when we encounter the simple dignity of their immediate presence, we suddenly ponder the mystery of human greatness.
>
> Perhaps this power springs from their dedication, their having subjected themselves successfully to the demanding discipline necessary to the mastery of their chosen art. Or, perhaps, it is a quality with which they are born as some are born with bright orange hair. Perhaps, though we think not, it is acquired, a technique of "presence." But whatever its source, it touches us as a rich abundance of human warmth and sympathy. Indeed, we feel that if the idea of aristocracy is more than mere class conceit, then these surely are our natural queens. For they enchant the eye as they caress the ear, and in their presence we sense the full, moony glory of womanhood in all its mystery—maid, matron and matriarch. They are the sincere ones whose humanity dominates the artifices of the art with which they stir us, and when they sing we have some notion of our better selves.
>
> Lotte Lehmann is one of these, and Marian Anderson. Both Madame Ernestine Schumann-Heink and Kathleen Ferrier possessed it. Nor is it limited to these mistresses of high art. Pastoria Pavon, "La Niña de Los Peines," the great flamenco singer, is another and so is Mahalia Jackson, the subject of this piece, who reminds us that while not all great singers possess this quality, those who do, no matter how obscure their origin, are soon claimed by the world as its own.
>
> —from "As the Spirit Moves Mahalia," *Shadow and Act*

Ellison celebrates Jackson as a musician as well as a singer. He glories in how she sings and relishes the memory of hearing her in person. What makes Ellison's own memorializing of Mahalia Jackson memorable is the care he takes with his language, the precision of his vocabulary and the elegance and grace of his sentences. Look, for example, at the shape and listen to the sound of his first two sentences. This kind of concern with the how as well as the what—with style as well as with thought—makes for outstanding writing.

In writing a research paper, you might trace the development of a performer's or composer's career. You could explore origins and influences, developments and continuities, changes and shifts of direction. For such an assignment, you need to identify a composer or performer that interests you (or about whom you would like to learn more) and begin with some questions to guide your reading, listening, and research. Questions such as "Why did the Beatles become a musical phenomenon in the 1960s?" or "What was the Beatles' musical legacy?" or "What makes Chopin's musical career and musical style distinctive?" Once you have a good question, your research paper can become your way of answering it. (For an extensive discussion of research writing, see Chapter 7.)

Here is an example of how one writer begins an essay on the music of the modern American composer Charles Ives. The writer is interested in the relationship of Ives's music to the ideas of the nineteenth-century American transcendentalists, including Ralph Waldo Emerson and Henry David Thoreau.

> Music, like literature, should present another world, but one to which we feel the tie. So Ives might have written had he known Melville's dictum; so he did often write in the language of his best music. The "other world" Ives's music represents is the world of nineteenth-century America, nostalgically remembered and lovingly recaptured. To suggest that Ives's music is closely tied to nineteenth-century America, however, is not to suggest that Ives acted as a curator of earlier American forms and myths. Nor is it to suggest that he was influenced by the compositional practices of nineteenth-century composers. The influence was philosophical rather than musical. From the philosophical currents circulating in mid-nineteenth-century America, Ives drew not a theory of composition, but a set of ideas, coherent if unsystematic, about the nature, forms and purposes of art and life.
>
> —from "Charles Ives and the Transcendentalists"
> Robert DiYanni, *Journal of American Culture*

In this paragraph, the writer lays out his claim that Ives's twentieth-century modern music owes a good deal to the nineteenth century. The writer makes clear, however, that this influence is less musical than philosophical. Later in the essay, the writer raises the specific question that drives the entire piece: "But what exactly did transcendentalism mean for Ives, and how did it find expression in his music?"

A similar kind of question motivates the student who wrote a research paper on the importance of Richard Wagner, the nineteenth-century German composer, best known for his music dramas. For now, here are some questions you can use to direct your thinking when writing about music:

- What strikes you most forcibly about the music—and the lyrics, if there are any?
- What instruments are used—and how many of each?
- Who is the composer? When was the work composed?
- Where does it fit in the composer's career?
- Why was it composed—for what kind of occasion?
- What is its musical genre or type?
- What is the structure of the work? How is it organized?
- What style and period is the work written in? What features of the work—its melodies, harmonies, rhythms, structure—reflect the characteristics of the period (such as the classical era)?
- Which features of the work mark it as particularly reflective of the composer who wrote it?
- How would you characterize its musical language—medieval, Renaissance, baroque, romantic?
- What does the work express or convey? What feelings and ideas does it communicate?

The Importance of Richard Wagner

by Karen Chen

"Of all the German figures of the nineteenth century, only Marx and Nietzsche had impacts equal to Wagner's on subsequent thought; like them, he could be attacked and parodied, but never ignored."

—Rey Longyear

Richard Wagner dominated the musical life of the second half of the nineteenth century as Beethoven dominated the musical world of the first half of the century (Schonberg 274). Both composers left their highly individual imprints on the music that would come after them. Both achieved greatness such that their works continue to serve as artistic monuments against which others' musical compositions are measured. Moreover, one might argue that Richard Wagner's operatic achievement compares with the achievement of Beethoven in symphonic music.

Unlike Beethoven, whose influence on future generations was confined to the realm of music, Richard Wagner's influence extended to art and politics. Also unlike Beethoven, whose works express a resilient optimism, a profound hope in human possibility, Wagner displays a more pessimistic attitude toward life. Influenced by the philosopher Arthur Schopenhauer, Wagner emphasizes the blind force of irrationality and passion that drive human behavior (Levy 251). His operas portray characters whose lives are made unhappy by circumstances they cannot control, as in his most famous opera, <u>Tristan and Isolde</u>, in which the two lovers are kept apart only to be united in death.

Wagner was born in 1813, in the northern German city of Leipzig, home also to Bach and Handel, of Beethoven and Brahms. Unlike these musicians, all of whom were musically precocious, and all of whom received extensive musical instruction in their youth, Wagner, when young, was more interested in literature than in music. Shakespeare, in fact, was his idol (Schonberg 275). Wagner did not begin the serious study of music until age fifteen, and he never mastered a musical instrument as Bach and Handel mastered the organ and Beethoven and Brahms the piano. Wagner was also largely self-taught, mostly through intense study of the works of Beethoven (Schonberg 275). In fact, later in life, Wagner explained that he had wanted to do for opera what Beethoven had done for symphonic music--to make it express a wide range of experience, and to have it achieve overwhelming emotional effects. Wagner's admiration for Beethoven can be heard in the following comment from his writings:

> The last symphony of Beethoven is the redemption of music from
> out of her peculiar element into the realm of universal
> art. . . . for upon it the perfect art work of the future alone
> can follow (Schonberg 275).

Wagner believed that he and he alone could compose this "perfect art work of the future," and he believed that it could not be an orchestral work since Beethoven's mighty ninth symphony could never be surpassed. Instead, Wagner would create a new kind of opera, which he called "music drama" (Levy 251).

II

Wagnerian music drama attempted to bring together song and instrumental music, dance and drama and poetry in a single unbroken stream of art. Wagner did not like the way any of these arts had developed in his time. He thought that song in opera had been reduced to the operatic aria, that dance had become only ballet, and that music in opera had become reduced to a secondary role of accompanying the singers (Longyear 165). His ambitious goal was to restore the importance of music in opera, to establish a better balance between orchestra and singers. His goal also included raising the quality of the texts of operas. He attempted this in part by finding his subjects in medieval legend and Nordic mythology and partly by writing his own librettos (Longyear 166).

In honoring his musical forefather, Beethoven, Wagner would use the orchestra to do more than simply provide beautiful accompaniments for operatic arias. Instead Wagner's operatic orchestral writing would arouse intense emotion, "comment" on stage action, and be associated with incidents in the plot and characters' behavior. One important and influential way that Wagner accomplished these goals was by using what were called "leitmotifs" (Levy 252). These musical motives were usually brief fragments of melody or rhythm that, when played, would remind the audience of particular characters and actions, somewhat in the way a movie or television theme triggers associations in the mind of the audience.

III

From all accounts, Wagner was not a very nice human being. He was arrogant, willful, pompous, and rude. He was also a liar, a deadbeat, and a sensualist (Levy 250). He has been further described as "a selfish ingrate, an egotistical profligate, and an obnoxious megalomaniac" (Frost and McClure). And he was nothing if not ambitious. His ambition eventually paid off, for even after producing a number of failed operas, and after living in political exile in Switzerland for eleven years, he secured the patronage of King Ludwig II of Bavaria, who enabled Wagner to acquire wealth, fame, and power. Most important for Wagner was that with Ludwig's support, he could fulfill his dream of establishing an annual festival at which his (and only his) music dramas would be performed. Wagner designed the auditorium and the sets for productions of his monumental operatic works, some of them lasting for as long as six hours.

Wagner's works include the comic <u>Die Meistersinger</u>, the popular <u>Lohengrin</u>, and the sensuous <u>Tristan and Isolde</u>, which influenced subsequent European musical style perhaps more than any work of the late nineteenth century. His tetralogy, <u>The Ring of the Niebelung</u>, which is generally considered his greatest work, includes four operas--<u>The Rhine Gold</u>, <u>The Valkyrie</u>, <u>Siegfried</u>, and <u>Twilight of the Gods</u>.

Because Wagner's music does not break easily into set pieces, it is difficult to illustrate his musical style. Complicating matters is that, like his great predecessor, Beethoven, his style developed and changed during his musical career, so much so that his music of the 1850s differs considerably from that of the 1870s (Schonberg 284). Nonetheless, something of the power Wagner could generate with an orchestra can be suggested with the Prelude to Act III of <u>Lohengrin</u>, especially in its opening and closing sections. The middle provides a brief hint of Wagner's lyrical style.

Alternatively, the mysterious quality of Wagner's music along with something of its relentless drive can be heard in his "Ride of the Valkyries" from his music drama <u>The Valkyrie</u>. Both of these excerpts provide examples of what might be called "Wagner's Greatest Hits." These popular selections, however, exist within a complex whole--the individual music dramas of which they are a part, and the entire range of Wagner's operatic output. As a result they can reflect only the slightest hint of his musical legacy. This legacy has been described best, perhaps, by the music historian Donald Grout, who sums up Wagner's enormous influence in this manner:

> Wagner's work affected all subsequent opera . . . His ideal of opera as a drama of significant content, with words, stage setting, visible action, and music all working in closest harmony toward the central purpose . . . was profoundly influential (Longyear 171).

IV

If Beethoven was the composer whose works crossed the bridge from the Classical style and outlook to a vision and style that is distinctively Romantic, Wagner is the composer whose greatest works epitomize that style and vision and bring it to its culmination. His music has long made such a powerful impression largely because its "sheer overwhelming power" creates in its listeners "that all-embracing state of ecstasy, at once sensuous and mystical, toward which all Romantic art had been striving" (Grout and Palisca 752). He also served as the "father of modern music", introducing chromaticism and pointing to atonality with his masterpiece Tristan and Isolde.

Wagner's stature as one of music's all-time prominent composers is beyond question, as is his position as one of the nineteenth century's most influential and provocative individuals. His impact extended beyond music into politics and philosophy, and he has done much to shape the world we know today.

Works Cited

Frost, Thomas and John McClure. Liner notes for The Wagner Album.
    New York: Columbia Records, MG 30300, n.d.
Grout, Donald J. and Claude V. Palisca. A History of Western Music,
    4th ed. New York: Norton, 1988.
Levy, Kenneth. Music: A Listener's Introduction. New York: Harper
    & Row, 1983.
Longyear, Rey M. Nineteenth-Century Romanticism in Music, 3rd ed.
    Englewood Cliffs, NJ: Prentice Hall, 1988.
Schonberg, Harold C. The Lives of the Great Composers, rev. ed.
    New York: Norton, 1981.

THE
HUMANITIES

6
Writing About Literature

Writing about literary works—stories, poems, or plays—is a common requirement in college courses. History instructors may require students to read and write about literature from the standpoint of their discipline. Novels and plays in particular often provide a window on the past and an understanding of social and cultural values of different times and places. Literary works are often included for study in psychology courses to illustrate the analysis of human motivation and various psychological complexes and behaviors, such as obsession, compulsion, and personality development. Philosophy courses sometimes include literary works to exemplify particular philosophical issues and movements, such as existentialism. Courses in health and medicine may include literature about doctors and nurses, as well as about aspects of disease. Because literature reflects the human condition, it makes a prime subject for many kinds of courses besides those specifically designed to teach its special qualities and features. This chapter offers a brief overview of the elements of literature—fiction, poetry, and drama—with a view to writing about stories, poems, and plays. The approach to writing about literary works provided here can help you understand literature better and write about it more confidently.

Before you can write about literary works with confidence, however, you need to understand something about how to interpret them. You have already had practice in interpretation, both in your previous study of literature and in Chapter 1. You can apply the approach to analysis and interpretation provided in this book—observing, connecting, inferring, and concluding—to writing about literary works.

WRITING ABOUT FICTION

Why write about fiction? Besides fulfilling a requirement, one reason is to find out what you think about a story or novel. Another is to read it more carefully. You may write about a work of fiction because it engages you. You may wish to praise its characters or style; you may want to argue with its implied ideas and values. You may find its action compelling.

Whatever your reasons for writing about a fictional work, a number of things happen when you do. First, you read it more attentively, noticing things you might overlook in a more casual reading. Second, you think more about what a particular work means and why you respond to it as you do. You also begin to acquire power over the works you write about, making them more meaningful to you.

When you write about a novel or short story, you may write for yourself, or you may write for others. In writing for yourself, you write to discover what you think. This type of writing takes casual forms, such as annotation and freewriting, which you practiced in Chapter 1. These less formal kinds of writing are useful for helping you focus on your reading of fiction. They can also serve as preliminary forms of writing for more formal essays and papers about fiction.

Annotation

When you annotate a text, you make notes about it, usually in the margins or at the top and bottom of pages—or both. You can make annotations within the text, as underlined words, circled phrases, bracketed sentences, or paragraphs. Your annotations may assume the form of arrows, question marks, and various other shorthand marks and symbols that you devise.

Annotating a literary work offers a convenient and relatively painless way to begin writing about it. Annotating starts you zeroing in on what you find interesting or think important. You can also annotate to signal details that puzzle or disconcert you.

Your markings help focus your attention and clarify your understanding. Your annotations can also save you time in rereading or studying a work. And they can also be used when you write a more extended essay about it.

EXERCISE

Select a short story or a novel to read, interpret, and write about. Begin the process by making some marginal annotations.

Freewriting

In freewriting, you explore a text to find out what you think about it and how you respond to it. When you freewrite, you may have only a preliminary idea of your idea and of your initial response to the work. You write about the work to see where your thinking takes you.

Freewriting leads you to explore your memories and experience as well as aspects of the text. When you freewrite, you may wander from the details of the story or novel you are writing about. In the process you may discover thoughts and feelings you didn't know you had or were only dimly aware of. You can use freewriting to explore these responses. You can also use freewriting to see where it leads you in thinking about the work itself.

EXERCISE

Reflect on the story you read and annotated for the previous exercise. Do ten minutes of freewriting about the work.

Analysis

Analysis is one of the most common ways of writing about fiction often required in college courses. In writing an analytical essay about a short story or a novel, your goal is to explain how one or more particular aspects or issues in the work contribute to its overall meaning. You might analyze a work's dialogue by explaining what the verbal exchanges between characters contribute to the story's meaning. You might analyze the characters in a story or novel to explain how their relationships reveal the story's theme or general idea.

One way to begin doing these kinds of analyses is by using the approach to interpretation explained in Chapter 1. You may wish to review the process described there: making observations, establishing connections, drawing inferences, and formulating a provisional, or tentative, conclusion.

EXERCISE

Make a list of observations and connections about the story you annotated and freewrote about for the previous exercises.

EXERCISE

Make a list of inferences based on those observations and connections.

Elements of Fiction

In reading fiction it is helpful to understand its basic elements: plot, character, setting, point of view, style, irony, symbol, and theme. Though each of these elements is described separately, the elements of a story or novel work together; each should be considered in relation to the work as a whole.

Plot is the action element in fiction, the arrangement of events that make up its story. Fictional plots often turn on a conflict between opposing forces which is resolved by the end of the work. Whether you are reading a novel, such as Jane Austen's *Pride and Prejudice,* or a short story by Ernest Hemingway, you typically expect a conflict that complicates the fictional work, pushing it toward a climax and ultimately a resolution.

Structure is related to plot. Plot is the sequence of unfolding action; structure is the design or form of the completed action. In examining plot we are concerned with how one action leads into or ties in with another. In examining structure, we look for patterns, the design the work possesses as a whole. A work's structure appears in recurring details of action, gesture, dialogue, and description. It appears in shifts and changes of direction and character relationships.

Character is the heart of fiction. We read often to find out what happens to them, how the plot works out for them, sometimes identifying with them. Characters allow readers to become caught up in their stories, becoming, for a time at least, intensely real, and perhaps affecting enough to influence readers' lives after their stories have ended.

Fictional characters also represent values that convey an author's attitude and ideas embodying the meaning of the work. Authors use the following techniques to convey such attitudes, ideas, and values about their characters:

- What characters say—their speech
- What characters do—their actions
- What characters think and feel—their consciousness
- How characters look—their dress and physical appearance
- What others think about them—judgments

Setting is the place or location of a fictional work's action, along with the time in which it occurs. For some writers, setting is essential to meaning. More than a simple backdrop for action, setting can provide a historical and cultural context that enhances readers' understanding of a writer's plots and characters.

Point of view concerns an author's choice of who tells the fictional story and how it is to be told. In objective point of view, the writer shows what happens without directly stating more than its action and dialogue imply. Stories with narrators who do not participate in the action are typically presented from a third-person point of view as compared with a first-person point of view, which characterizes stories with participant narrators.

Whether they use a first- or a third-person narrator, writers must decide how much to let the narrator know about the characters. Narrators who know everything about a work's characters are "omniscient" or all-knowing; narrators who know only some things about the characters possess "limited omniscience."

A writer's choice of point of view affects our response to the characters. That response is affected by the fictional narrator, especially by the degree of the narrator's knowledge, the objectivity of the narrator's responses, and the degree of the narrator's participation in the action. It is also affected by the extent to which we find the narrator a trustworthy guide to a work's characters and action. It is our responsibility as readers to determine a narrator's reliability and to estimate the truth of the narrator's disclosures.

Style refers to a writer's choice of words, and to his or her arrangement of them in sentences and longer units of discourse. Style is the writer's verbal identity, as unmistakable as his or her face or voice. Reflecting their individuality, writers' styles convey their unique ways of seeing the world.

Aspects of style to consider when analyzing a fictional work include diction (the writer's choice of words), syntax (the order of words in sentences), imagery, figurative language, selection of detail, pacing of action, and the amount, nature, and purpose of description. Recognizing the particular qualities of a writer's style is one way to appreciate his or her unique literary achievement.

Irony is not as much an element of fiction as a pervasive quality in it. Irony may appear in fiction in three ways: in the work's language (or style), in its incidents (or plot), or in its point of view. Writers employ verbal irony to convey a character's limited understanding. They employ irony of circumstance or situation to reveal discrepancies between what seems to be and what is, or between what is expected and what actually happens. Writers also use dramatic irony to reveal the difference between what characters know and what readers know, sometimes directing our responses by letting us see things their characters do not.

Some writers exploit the discrepancy between what readers and characters know to establish an ironic vision in a work. An ironic vision is an overall tone that results from the multiple examples of irony that a work includes. Jane Austen's *Pride and Prejudice* reveals an ironic quality right from its opening sentence: "It is a truth universally acknowledged, that a single man in possession of a good fortune, must be in want of a wife." Jane Austen's sentence actually says the opposite of what it means. Single men of means, more often than not, in her time and in ours, are not often in search of wives. In fact, the reverse is usually the case: single men of means are sought out as prospective husbands, largely because of their money.

We can feel more confident about the ironic quality of Austen's first sentence when we examine it in relation to the sentence that follows it: "However little known the feelings or views of such a man may be on his first entering a neighborhood, this truth is so well fixed in the minds of the surrounding families, that he is considered as the rightful property of some one or other of their daughters." The ironic quality of this sentence involves its reversal of the conventional image of a woman being the "property" of a man. Its humor resides partly in this reversal and partly in its assertion of families' and their daughters' "rights" to such an eligible man. Taken together, these opening sentences establish the ironic tone for the novel.

Symbols in fiction are objects, actions, or events that convey meaning. The meaning of a symbolic object, action, or event extends beyond its literal significance. Yet how do we know if a particular detail is symbolic? How do we decide whether we should look beyond the literal meaning of a dialogue or the literal value of an object or an action? Although we cannot always be certain about the significance of any detail, we can be alert to its possible symbolic overtones.

The following questions can serve as guidelines for thinking about symbols in literary works:

- How important is the object, action, gesture, or dialogue? Does it appear more than once? Does it occur at a climactic moment? Is it described in detail?
- Does a symbolic interpretation make sense? Does it fit in with a literal or common-sense explanation?
- What objections might be raised against a symbolic interpretation?

Theme refers to a story's idea formulated as a generalization. The theme of a fable is its moral; the theme of a parable is its teaching; the theme of a novel or story is its implied view of life and conduct. Fictional themes in novels and stories are most often obliquely presented rather than directly stated. More often than not, theme is less presented than implied; it is abstracted by readers from details of character and action that constitute the fictional story.

WRITING ABOUT POETRY

You write about poems for the same reasons you write about stories, with many of the same results. In writing about a poem, you tend to read it more attentively and think harder about its meaning. In writing about a poem for yourself, to discover what you think, you can use the same strategies as for writing about fiction, including annotation and freewriting. As with writing about fiction, these less formal kinds of writing are useful for helping you focus on your reading of poems, in studying for tests about poetry, and as preliminary forms of writing when you write more formal essays and papers about poetry.

Analysis

In writing an analytical essay about a poem, your goal is to explain how one or more particular aspects or issues in the work contribute to its overall meaning. You might analyze, for example, a poem's speaker and situation, its diction or imagery, its syntax, structure, sound, and/or sense. In the process, your goal would be to see what any or all of the poetic elements contribute to the meaning of the poem as a whole.

In addition to analyzing these and other poetic elements in a single poem, you might also write to compare two poems, perhaps by focusing on their symbolism, sound effects, rhythm and meter, structure, or figures of speech. Or, instead of focusing on literary elements, you might write to see how a particular critical perspective, such as a feminist or reader-response perspective, illuminates a poem.

Elements of Poetry

In some ways, reading poetry is much like reading fiction. Readers observe details of action and language, make connections and inferences based on the details they observe, and draw conclusions about the work's meaning or theme. Yet there is something different about reading poems. The difference, although one more of degree than of kind, involves being more attentive to the connotations of words, more receptive to the expressive qualities of sound and rhythm in line and stanza, more discerning about details of syntax and punctuation. Poetry is typically denser and more concentrated, more compressed than fiction. This is almost always true of lyric poetry, and it is often the case with epic, narrative, and dramatic poetry as well.

Diction refers to a poet's choice of words. In reading any poem, it is necessary to know what the words mean, but it is equally important to understand what the words imply or suggest. Knowing the words' denotations or dictionary meanings is necessary but not sufficient. Attention to the *connotations,* or associations and suggestions, of a poem's language is equally important for understanding. Consider the opening stanza of the following poem by the British Romantic poet William Wordsworth:

> I wandered lonely as a cloud
> That floats on high o'er vales and hills,
> When all at once I saw a crowd,
> A host of golden daffodils;
> Beside the lake, beneath the trees,
> Fluttering and dancing in the breeze.

The "I" of this poem describes himself as "lonely," which suggests not only that he is literally alone but also that he experiences that single state unhappily. When a person is lonely, he or she typically does not want to be alone. That is one of the connotations of the word *lonely.*

Wordsworth uses the word *crowd* to describe the daffodils, an unusual word in this context because *crowd* refers more often to people than to flowers. The connotations of *crowd* suggest more than a large number of people. They also carry the sense of not being alone and of not being lonely. The word *crowd* thus connotes, or suggests, the opposite of *lonely.* A third word in these lines is also rich with connotation: *golden,* which describes the color of the daffodils. If the poet had described the daffodils as "yellow" rather than as "golden," he would have lost the connotations of wealth and value that the word *golden* conveys. Considering the connotations of these and other words enables you to better understand the poem's theme and the resources of language the poet employs in expressing it.

Imagery.   Poems are grounded in the concrete and the specific—in details that stimulate our senses—for it is through our senses that we perceive the world. When specific details appear in poems, they are called *"images."* An *image* is a concrete representation of a sense impression, feeling, or idea. Images may appeal to the senses of sight, hearing, touch, taste, or smell.

Poetry describes specific things, for example, daffodils, fires, and finches' wings. Typically, poets describe such things in specific terms: the color of the daffodils, the glare of the fire, the beating of the finches' wings. From these and other specific details readers derive an understanding of the meaning of poems and the feelings they convey.

Consider the images in the second and third stanzas of Wordsworth's poem:

> Continuous as the stars that shine
> And twinkle on the milky way,
> They stretched in never-ending line
> Along the margin of a bay:
> Ten thousand saw I at a glance,
> Tossing their heads in sprightly dance.
>
> The waves beside them danced; but they
> Outdid the sparkling waves in glee;
> A poet could not but be gay,
> In such a jocund company:
> I gazed—and gazed—but little thought
> What wealth the show to me had brought:

Wordsworth emphasizes the imagery of light in describing how the stars "shine" and "twinkle." He continues this image in the next stanza's image of the "sparkling waves." The water reflects the light of the sun, by which the poet connects the two stanzas' images, linking the sky's milky way of "continuous" stars and the bay's water with its glittering waves.

Figurative Language.   Language can be classified as literal or figurative. Literal language conveys the meaning of the words themselves; figurative language conveys meaning that differs from the actual meanings of the words. Of the more than 250 types of figures of speech, among the most important for poetry are metaphor and simile. The heart of both these figures of speech is a comparison between normally unrelated things.

Simile establishes its comparison by the use of the words *like, as,* or *as though.* Metaphor uses no such verbal clue. When Wordsworth writes, "I wandered lonely as a cloud," he uses a simile to emphasize the speaker's isolation. The simile limits the comparison between speaker and cloud to this one aspect. When Wordsworth writes in the poem's final stanza that the daffodils he once saw "flash" upon the "inward eye," he uses "flash" as a metaphor for remembering—recollecting the flowers in his "inward eye," a metaphor for memory. When the speaker "sees" the daffodils in his "inward eye," he realizes the great "wealth" they have brought him. This "wealth" is figurative; Wordsworth uses "wealth" as a metaphor for joy:

> For oft, when on my couch I lie
> In vacant or in pensive mood,
> They flash upon that inward eye
> Which is the bliss of solitude;
> And then my heart with pleasure fills,
> And dances with the daffodils.

Symbols in poems are objects that stand for something beyond themselves—feelings, experiences, or abstract ideas. A rose can represent beauty or love or mortality; a lily can stand for purity or innocence. Ashes can represent death; birds can symbolize freedom. Light and darkness can stand for life and death, knowledge and ignorance, joy and sorrow.

The meaning of a poetic symbol is controlled by its context. Whether fire symbolizes lust, rage, destruction, or purification (or nothing beyond itself) can only be determined within the context of a particular poem. Nor is there any limit to how many symbolic meanings an object, character, or gesture may possess.

Deciding on the symbolic significance of a poetic detail is not an easy matter. Even when we are fairly confident that something is symbolic, it is not often a simple task to determine just what it represents. Like any inferential connection made while interpreting poetry, the decision to view something as symbolic depends in large part on whether the poetic context invites and rewards a symbolic interpretation. In Wordsworth's poem, we might say that the daffodils symbolize the power of nature to restore a person's good feeling. For it is the memory of seeing the daffodils that lifts the spirits of the poem's speaker.

Syntax, which comes from a Greek word meaning "to arrange together," refers to the grammatical structure of words in sentences and their deployment in longer units. Syntax is the order or sequence of words in a sentence. Poets occasionally alter the normal syntactic order, as does Emily Dickinson in the following stanza from "Tell all the Truth but tell it slant":

> Tell all the Truth but tell it slant—
> Success in Circuit lies
> Too bright for our infirm Delight
> The Truth's superb surprise.

Dickinson inverts normal syntax in the second line after establishing it in line 1. She then alters the word order more dramatically by reversing the grammatical sentence order of lines 3–4. The difference is apparent in the following reconstruction of Dickinson's lines in a more conventional syntactic arrangement:

> Tell all the Truth but tell it slant
> [For] Success lies in Circuit
> The superb surprise [of] Truth's [is]
> Too bright for our infirm Delight.

What the more conventional syntactic arrangement loses most dramatically is the steady rhythm that beats in Dickinson's original lines, which are arranged in alternating units of eight and six syllables.

The most familiar element of poetry is *rhyme,* the matching of final vowel and consonant sounds in two or more words, usually at the ends of poetic lines. For the poet, rhyme is a challenge; for the reader, rhyme is a pleasure. Part of its pleasure for the reader is in anticipating and hearing a poem's echoing song. Part of its challenge for the poet is in rhyming naturally, without forcing the rhythm, the syntax, or the sense. When the challenge is met successfully, the poem is a pleasure to listen to; it sounds natural to the ear, and its rhyme aids those who would remember it.

Robert Frost's "Stopping by Woods on a Snowy Evening" is one such rhyming success. Its music is best heard when read aloud.

Here is the opening stanza:

> Whose woods these are I think I know.
> His house is in the village, though;
> He will not see me stopping here
> To watch his woods fill up with snow.

Three of the stanza's four lines rhyme—1, 2, and 4, with line 3 the lone un-rhymed line. But Frost does something special with this line. He makes its unrhymed sound the rhyming sound of the next stanza, thereby creating a link between the first and second stanzas.

Structure. Basically, poetic structure can be described as open or closed. Poems written in open structures or open forms do not follow a prescribed pattern of rhyme or stanzaic patterning. They are freer, looser, and less con-strained than poems written in closed or fixed forms. Poems in closed forms adhere more closely to prescribed requirements concerning line length, rhyme, and stanzaic structure.

An example of a closed form is the sonnet, which is typically written according to one of two common patterns: the Shakespearean sonnet and the Petrarchan sonnet. Both kinds of sonnets are fourteen lines long with ten syllables per line arranged in alternating stressed syllables. The Shake-spearean, or English, sonnet divides into three four-line quatrains and a concluding couplet. Its rhyme scheme is abab cdcd efef gg. The Petrarchan or Italian sonnet consists of an eight-line octave and a six-line sestet, often rhyming abba abba cde cde.

Not every poem in closed form, however, follows as strict a set of for-mal requirements as the sonnet, as the following poem by the modern American poet Langston Hughes indicates:

My People

The night is beautiful,
So the faces of my people.

The stars are beautiful,
So the eyes of my people.

Beautiful, also, is the sun.
Beautiful, also, are the souls of my people.

Hughes's poem uses parallel structure throughout. Lines 1 and 3 echo each other structurally. Lines 2 and 4 do the same, as do lines 5 and 6. Although parallelism is the primary structural device of the poem, there is another structure that accompanies it. The odd-numbered lines identify aspects of nature: night, stars, and sun. The corresponding even-numbered lines fo-cus on the human dimension, specifically on how black African Americans are considered "beautiful," a word that appears in each couplet or two-line stanza. In addition, the poem describes a kind of progression from dark to light to greater light—from the darkness of night, to the stars with their reflected light, to the sun with its self-generated light. This progression is paralleled by that describing Hughes's people—first their faces, then their eyes, and finally their souls. The progression moves from outside to inside, external to internal, surface to depth. Seeing the structural design of Hughes's poem helps readers appreciate his poetic accomplishment while also enhancing their understanding of the poem's meaning.

Theme.   As with fiction, theme in poetry involves an abstraction or generalization drawn from the details of a work. Theme refers to the idea of a poem, its meaning and significance. One of the dangers of deciding on the theme of a poem is in oversimplifying its meaning, perhaps reducing a complex idea to a cliché. Like other forms of literature, poems can contain multiple themes. Considering a poem's themes leads us toward understanding what it signifies—what it says and suggests about life.

WRITING ABOUT DRAMA

You may write about a play for some of the same reasons you write about poems and stories. You may wish to read it more carefully, you find that it engages you, or you may need to review a play for the school newspaper. Still another reason is that you may simply be required to do so as a course assignment.

When you write about a play, you may write for yourself or you may write for others. Writing for yourself, to discover what you think, often takes casual forms such as annotation and freewriting. These less formal kinds of writing are as useful for helping you focus on your reading of plays as they are for poems and stories. They can also serve as preliminary forms of writing when you write more formal essays and papers.

Double-Column Notebook

Another way of writing for yourself, informally, is to use the double-column notebook. To create a double-column notebook, divide a page in half vertically (or open a notebook so that you face two blank pages side by side). On one side *take* notes, summarizing the scene's situation, action, and ideas. On the other side, *make* notes, responding to what you summarized on the opposite side. On the responding side, record your thinking about what you read. Ask questions; speculate; make connections.

Here is an example of the double-column notebook applied to a short play, *Andre's Mother,* reprinted below.

Notes	Comments
The balloons—symbols of soul ascending to heaven.	Why balloons? They're light— they ascend. Air inside = breath, spirit—soul?
Penny indicates Andre was gay.	Penny is closest to her gay brother.
Did she desire him? She was attracted.	Seems natural about it all.
The father remembers Andre affectionately, warmly.	Arthur—appreciates Andre's help in understanding Cal as gay.
Andre's mother doesn't speak a word.	Cal lectures Andre's mother—remote— Guilty?? in denying her son??

Terrence McNally

Andre's Mother

CHARACTERS
CAL
ARTHUR
PENNY
ANDRE'S MOTHER

> *Four people enter. They are nicely dressed and carry white helium-filled balloons on a string. They are* CAL, *a young man;* ARTHUR, *his father;* PENNY, *his sister; and* ANDRE'S MOTHER.

CAL: You know what's really terrible? I can't think of anything terrific to say. Goodbye. I love you. I'll miss you. And I'm supposed to be so great with words!

PENNY: What's that over there?

ARTHUR: Ask your brother.

CAL: It's a theatre. An outdoor theatre. They do plays there in the summer. Shakespeare's plays. (*To* ANDRE'S MOTHER.) God, how much he wanted to play Hamlet. It was his greatest dream. I think he would have sold his soul to play it. He would have gone to Timbuktu to have another go at that part. The summer he did it in Boston, he was so happy!

PENNY: Cal, I don't think she . . . ! It's not the time. Later.

ARTHUR: Your son was a . . . the Jews have a word for it . . .

PENNY: (*Quietly appalled.*) Oh my God!

ARTHUR: Mensch, I believe it is and I think I'm using it right. It means warm, solid, the real thing. Correct me if I'm wrong.

PENNY: Fine, dad, fine. Just quit while you're ahead.

ARTHUR: I won't say he was like a son to me. Even my son isn't always like a son to me. I mean . . . ! In my clumsy way, I'm trying to say how much I liked Andre. And how much he helped me to know my own boy. Cal was always my two hands full but Andre and I could talk about anything under the sun. My wife was very fond of him, too.

PENNY: Cal, I don't understand about the balloons.

CAL: They represent the soul. When you let go, it means you're letting his soul ascend to Heaven. That you're willing to let go. Breaking the last earthly ties.

PENNY: Does the Pope know about this?

ARTHUR: Penny!

PENNY: Andre loved my sense of humor. Listen, you can hear him laughing. (*She lets go of her white balloon.*) So long, you glorious, wonderful, I-know-what-Cal-means-about-words . . . *man!* God forgive me for wishing you were straight every time I laid eyes on you. But if any man was going to have you, I'm glad it was my brother! Look how fast it went up. I bet that means something. Something terrific.

ARTHUR: (ARTHUR *lets his balloon go.*) Goodbye. God speed.

PENNY: Cal?

CAL: I'm not ready yet.

PENNY: Okay. We'll be over there. Come on, pop, you can buy your little girl a Good Humor.

ARTHUR: They still make Good Humor?

PENNY: Only now they're called Dove Bars and they cost 12 dollars.

PENNY *takes* ARTHUR *off.* CAL *and* ANDRE'S MOTHER *stand with their balloons.*)

CAL: I wish I knew what you were thinking. I think it would help me. You know almost nothing about me and I only know what Andre told me about you. I'd always had it in my mind that one day we would be friends, you and me. But if you didn't know about Andre and me . . . If this hadn't happened, I wonder if he would have ever told you. When he was so sick, if I asked him once I asked him a thousand times, tell her. She's your mother. She won't mind. But he was so afraid of hurting you and of your disapproval. I don't know which was worse. (*No response. He sighs.*) God, how many of us live in this city because we don't want to hurt our mothers and live in mortal terror of their disapproval. We lose ourselves here. Our lives aren't furtive, just our feelings toward people like you are! A city of fugitives from our parent's scorn or heartbreak. Sometimes he'd seem a little down and I'd say, "What's the matter, babe?" and this funny sweet, sad smile would cross his face and he'd say, "Just a little homesick, Cal, just a little bit." I always accused him of being a country boy just playing at being a hot shot, sophisticated New Yorker. (*He sighs.*) It's bullshit. It's all bullshit. (*Still no response.*) Do you remember the comic strip Little Lulu? Her mother had no name, she was so remote, so formidable to all the children. She was just Lulu's mother. "Hello, Lulu's Mother," Lulu's friends would say. She was almost anonymous in her remoteness. You remind me of her. Andre's Mother. Let me answer the questions you can't ask and then I'll leave you alone and you won't ever have to see me again. Andre died of AIDS. I don't know how he got it. I tested negative. He died bravely. You would have been proud of him. The only thing that frightened him was you. I'll have everything that was his sent to you. I'll pay for it. There isn't much. You should have come up the summer he played Hamlet. He was magnificent. Yes, I'm bitter. I'm bitter I've lost him. I'm bitter what's happening. I'm bitter even now, after all this, I can't reach you. I'm beginning to feel your disapproval and it's making me ill. (*He looks at his balloon.*) Sorry, old friend. I blew it. (*He lets go of the balloon.*) Good night, sweet prince, and flights of angels sing thee to thy rest! (*Beat.*) Goodbye, Andre's Mother. (*He goes.* ANDRE'S MOTHER *stands alone holding her white balloon. Her lip trembles. She looks on the verge of breaking down. She is about to let go of the balloon when she pulls it down to her. She looks at it a while before she gently kisses it. She lets go of the balloon. She follows it with her eyes as it rises and rises. The lights are beginning to fade.* ANDRE'S MOTHER'S *eyes are still on the balloon. Blackout.*)

(*1988*)

Analysis

In writing an analytical essay about a play or a scene from a play, your goal is to explain how one or more particular aspects or issues in the work or the scene contribute to its overall meaning. In analyzing the dialogue in a scene from a play, your goal would be to explain what the verbal exchanges between characters contribute to the play's meaning and to its effect on the audience. You might analyze the imagery of a play to see what that imagery suggests about a character's perspective or the author's attitude toward the characters or the action. Or you might analyze its plot or staging to see how the playwright's manipulation of action creates tension and conflict, humor and irony.

Elements of Drama

Plot and Structure.   One of the reasons we read plays is to discover what happens, to see how particular consequences result from specific observable actions. We become engaged by a play's story line and remain held by its twists and turns, until the playwright resolves its complications. The details of action, or incidents, in a well-organized play form a unified structure. This unified structure of a play's incidents is called its *plot.*

It is important to realize that a dramatic plot is not merely a series of haphazardly occurring incidents. It is, rather, a carefully arranged series of causally related incidents. The incidents of the plot, that is, must be connected in such a way that one gives rise to another or directly results from another. And of course the playwright shapes and arranges the incidents of the plot to do precisely these things.

Besides being unified, a good plot will also be economical. This means that all the play's incidents contribute to its overall meaning and effect. No actions included in the play are extraneous or unnecessary. The economy of a play's plot distinguishes it from everyday life, in which a multitude of minor actions mingle indiscriminately with significant related incidents. Dramatists, however, fit together the actions of their plays in meaningful ways.

The *exposition* of a play presents background necessary for the development of the plot. The *rising action* includes the separate incidents that "complicate" the plot and build toward its most dramatic moment. These incidents often involve conflicts either between characters or within them, conflicts that lead to a crisis. The point of crisis toward which the play's action builds is called its *climax.* Following this high point of intensity in the play is the *falling action,* in which there is a relaxation of emotional intensity and a gradual resolution of the various strands of the plot in the play's *denouement.* This last is a French word that refers to the untying of a knot.

The plot of *Andre's Mother,* for example, involves a few simple actions—conversation about a dead man, the release of the helium-filled balloons in an unusual memorial ceremony, and a lecture critical of the dead man's mother, given by his gay lover. The crisis, climax, and denouement all occur during this speech, which occupies half the length of the brief play and immediately after, as the mother kisses her balloon and then releases it.

Whether playwrights use a traditional plot or vary the formula, they control our expectations about what is happening through their arrangement and structure of incidents. They decide when to present information and when to withhold it, when to arouse our curiosity and when to satisfy it. By arranging incidents, a dramatist may create suspense, evoke laughter, cause anxiety, or elicit surprise. One of our main sources of pleasure in plot, in fact, is surprise, whether we are shown something we didn't expect or whether we see *how* something will happen even when we may know *what* will happen. Surprise often follows suspense, thus fulfilling our need to find out what happens as we await the resolution of a play's action.

In considering our expectations and response to the developing action of a play, we approach the concept of plot less as a schematic diagram of a play's completed action and more as an evolving series of experiences we undergo as we read or view it. For our emotional experience in reading a play is an important aspect of the play's meaning for us.

Another dimension of a play's structure is the way it satisfies our need for order and form. Besides considering how a play is structured to affect us emotionally, we can also consider ways it exhibits formal or artistic design. In the first instance we attend to the theatrical and psychological aspect of structure; in the second, to its aesthetic dimension. Both contribute to our experience of drama. Both aspects of structure contribute to the meanings of plays.

We can be alert for a play's structure even as we read it for the first time, primarily by paying attention to repeated elements and recurring details—of action and gesture, of dialogue and description—and to shifts in direction and changes of focus. Repetition signals important connections and relationships in the play, relationships between characters, connections among ideas. Shifts in direction are often signaled by such visual or aural clues as a change of scene or the appearance of additional characters. They may also be indicated by changes in the time or place of the action and by alterations in the play's language or tempo.

In *Andre's Mother,* for example, we notice a shift from brief exchanges of dialogue among the characters to a single long speech that Cal gives to Andre's mother. We notice, too, that all the characters speak except for Andre's mother. There is a shift as well in her reaction—as she is about to break down in tears—and in the way she pulls her balloon down and kisses it before releasing it.

Character and Conflict.   If we read plays for their plots—to find out what happens—we also read them to discover the fates of their characters. We become interested in dramatic characters for varying, even contradictory, reasons. They may remind us in some ways of ourselves; they may appeal to us because they differ from us. They may represent alternative directions we might have taken, alternative decisions we might have made. And although fictional characters cannot be directly equated with actual people, they are usually recognizably human, and as such, subject to the changing conditions of circumstance.

Characters bring plays to life. First and last we attend to characters—to how they look and what their appearance tells us about them; to what they say and what their manner of saying expresses; to what they do and how their actions reveal who they are and what they stand for. We may come to know dramatic characters and respond to them in ways we come to know and respond to actual people, all the while realizing that characters are imaginative constructions, literary imitations of human beings. Yet even though characters in plays are not real people, their human dimension is impossible to ignore, because actors portray them, and their human qualities typically engage us. Nonetheless, it is helpful to remain mindful of the distinction between dramatic characters and actual people, so that we do not expect them always to behave realistically and so that we do not expect playwrights to tell us more about them than we need to know for the meaning of the play.

Character is the companion of plot; the plot of a play involves the actions of its characters. Another way of defining plot, in fact, is simply as characters in action (or interaction). And in the same way that a play's plot must be unified, so must a character be coherent. This means that all aspects of the character—speech, dress, gesture, movement—must work together to suggest a focused and unified whole. Our sense of a character's coherence, however, derives mainly from his or speech and actions. From these we gain a sense of who characters are and what they are like. But even though speech and action are the primary indicators of character, our sense of characters' identity and personality are derived essentially from four things: (1) their actions—what they do; (2) their words—what they say and how they say it; (3) their physical attributes—what they look like; and (4) the responses of other characters to them—what others say or do about them.

Even as short a play as *Andre's Mother* gives us an opportunity to assess the characters and understand their relationships via their words and actions. We acquire hints of understanding of Andre and his relationship with each of the other characters—his lover, Cal; his sister, Penny; his father, Arthur; and his mother, who is otherwise unnamed, to suggest, as Cal intimates, her remoteness.

Dialogue and Monologue.   This discussion of character and conflict brings us to a critical aspect of dramatic characters—their speech or dialogue. Although generally we use the word *dialogue* to refer to all the speech of a play, strictly speaking, "dialogue" involves two speakers and "monologue," one. An important dramatic convention of dialogue in the broader sense is the use of a soliloquy to express a character's state of mind. A *soliloquy* is a speech given by a character as if alone, even though other characters may be on stage. A soliloquy represents a character's thoughts so the audience can know what he or she is thinking at a given moment. Soliloquies should be distinguished from *asides,* which are comments made directly to the audience in the presence of other characters, but without those other characters' hearing what is said. A soliloquy, moreover, is typically a speech and is thus longer than an aside, which is usually a brief utterance.

Dialogue is more than simply the words characters utter. It is also itself action, since characters' words have the power to affect each other and the audience. Words in drama initiate events and effect change. Dialogue, moreover, is an important index of character, not only in what characters say about themselves and each other, but in their manner or way of expressing what they say. This concern with characters' language is crucial, whether we attend plays in the theater or imagine them performed in the theaters of our minds.

Aspects of dialogue are admittedly much harder to discern in a silent reading of the play. Some would contend that they are impossible to hear. Perhaps. But with an imaginative effort and a willingness to read aloud on occasion, we can begin to hear how much meaning and feeling the dialogue conveys. Better yet, we can go to the theater and hear the drama for ourselves.

In imagining how the lines in *Andre's Mother* might be spoken, we try to hear the tones of voice each of the actors uses to portray his or her character. For such a brief play there are a variety of voice tones and inflections the characters employ in their snatches of conversation with one another. In the long speech Cal makes before Andre's mother, we would listen for both the predominant tone of accusation and for shifts in tone that convey his changing feelings as he speaks.

Setting and Staging.   The action of a play, like that of any fictional work, occurs in a particular place and time. We call this spatial and temporal location its *setting.* Although some plays are set approximately in the times and places of their composition, more often than not a play's setting departs significantly from the time and place of its composition. The immediate world of a playwright is not often directly represented in the environment and milieu in which he or she sets a particular play. This does not mean, however, that there cannot be important connections between the playwright's immediate milieu and the possibly very different time and place of the play's action. Sometimes, in fact, particularly in political plays (and often in Shakespeare), historical events of earlier times reflect social and political situations of the playwright's own time. Shakespeare's London is clearly not the world depicted in *Hamlet,* yet the importance of monarchy, central to the play, was important in sixteenth-century England. The critical thing, though, is not the literal identity of a playwright's milieu with that of a given play, but rather the impression the setting makes on us, what it contributes to our understanding and experience of the play.

When we attend a play (and when we read one) the first thing we see is the stage set, the physical objects that suggest the world of the play. The stage set is usually indicated by the playwright, though the degree of detail and specificity of this rendering vary from one playwright to another, and from one literary period to another.

The setting for *Andre's Mother* is not specifically indicated, except that it is outdoors. The stage directions are sparse until the very end, when the mother's actions are described in detail. The set for this play leaves room for directors and stage managers to decide just how to represent its world. There is less room for such decisions, however, in plays with very explicit directions for stage sets, such as those for plays such as Anton Chekhov's *The Cherry Orchard* or Arthur Miller's *Death of a Salesman.*

The setting of a play is one element of its *staging,* or the spectacle a play presents in performance. Staging in general refers to all the visual detail of a play. It includes the positions of actors onstage (sometimes referred to as *blocking*); their postures, gestures, movements, and expressions *(stage business);* the scenic background; the props and costumes; the lighting and sound effects.

A playwright's stage directions will sometimes help us imagine such things as we read. Regardless, an increased imaginative alertness to the sights and sounds of a play, although no substitute for direct physical apprehension, can nonetheless help us approximate the experience of a dramatic performance. It can also enhance our appreciation of the dramatist's craftsmanship and increase our understanding of the play.

Thought and Theme.   From examining the various elements of a play we derive a sense of its significance and meaning. One of the dangers of reading drama without attending sufficiently to its theatrical dimension is that we may reduce its meaning to a single unnecessarily simplified and overly generalized statement of idea. We use the word *theme* to designate the main idea or point of a play stated as a generalization. Because formulating the theme of a play involves abstracting from it a generalizable idea, theme inevitably moves away from the very details of character and action that give the play its life. This is not to suggest that we should not attempt to identify a central idea or set of ideas from plays, but only that we should be aware of the limitations in doing so.

First, we should distinguish the ideas that may appear *in* a play from the idea *of* a play. The meaning of a play—its central, governing, or animating idea—is rarely identifiable as an explicit social, political, or philosophical idea manifest in the dialogue. Rather, a play's idea or meaning is almost always implicit, bound up with and derivable from the play's structure, character interactions, dialogue, and staging. Because the theme of a play grows out of the relationships among its concrete details, any statement of it that omits significant aspects of a play's dramatic elements will inevitably represent a limitation and a distortion of the play's meaning. Any statement of theme, in fact, inevitably only approximates a play's meaning rather than fully characterizing or embodying it.

As readers of drama, we tend to reach for theme as a way of organizing our responses to a play, as a way of coming to terms with what it implies about how human beings live. At times we emphasize our personal responses, our emotional reactions to what the play dramatizes. At times we seize on an intellectual response based on observations of its action and on inferences drawn from connections we establish from among its details. At times we look at what the play is; at times we feel what the play does. For the meaning of any play is ultimately more than any statement of theme, any series of words and sentences that we employ to describe it. Our experience, our moment-by-moment engagement with the play on stage or page, constitutes its meaning for us.

The theme of *Andre's Mother* concerns the tensions that exist in families whose children fear their parents' disapproval of their sexual identities. Or we might say that the play portrays the sense of loss and grief that exists in families when they realize too late that they shut their homosexual children out of their lives. An additional theme concerns the inability of language to express the full extent of people's feelings about these things and about one another. This is suggested forcefully by the silence of Andre's mother but is indicated in earlier remarks about the inadequacy of words to capture feelings.

The following sample essay focuses on the theme of *Andre's Mother,* especially on its ideas about human relationships as they are affected by AIDS. The title character, Andre's mother, is pivotal and thus receives a good deal of attention, as does the character Andre, who has died of AIDS.

The Silent Grief of Andre's Mother
by Andrea Martinez

The title of Terrence McNally's brief one-act play directs our
attention to its two central characters, Andre, a young homosexual man,
and his mother, whose name is not given in the play. By withholding the
name of Andre's mother, the playwright stresses that what is important
is the relationship between mother and son, her all-important role as
mother. This, of course, is a significant problem because Andre's
mother seems to have neglected her son, by ignoring his homosexuality.

Andre himself, the center of other characters' attention in the
play, is characterized by means of their comments about him. We learn
a good deal about him, perhaps most importantly that he was hurt by his
mother's neglect and by her unwillingness to accept him for what he
was--a gay man. It is apparent that Andre could not act naturally and
be at ease with his mother. Her disapproval of his and his lover
Cal's lifestyle prevented mother and son from developing a warm and
deep relationship.

Andre is compared to the character of Shakespeare's Hamlet at one
point. Perhaps, like Hamlet, Andre felt unhappy about his mother's
behavior. Hamlet's mother, Queen Gertrude, married her husband's
brother after he, Claudius, had murdered Hamlet's father. Hamlet was
greatly upset over both the fact of his mother's remarriage and the
speed with which she remarried. Like Queen Gertrude, Andre's mother
seems selfish in placing her own interests above those of her son.

Although Andre's mother does not speak a single line in the play,
she receives a good deal of attention, at first indirectly through
comments made about her son, and then later, in a long and bitter speech
that Andre's lover Cal makes criticizing her. Most important of all,
perhaps, is that she says nothing in response to Cal's speech. This
might indicate that she has nothing to say to Cal any more than she had
to Andre while he was alive. Or it might indicate that she feels guilty
as charged with what Cal is saying.

Her behavior at the end of the play reveals the deep sorrow she
feels at the loss of her son and probably as well at her neglect of him
while he was alive. The stage directions describe her as ready to break
down before she kisses the balloon, as if to offer a tender goodbye to

her son while apparently asking him for forgiveness. She is alone on
the stage at the end of the play, lost in her memories of her son. Even
at the end her grief remains silent, suggesting perhaps that she has not
yet found the words to express the depth of her sorrow. The silent
grief of Andre's mother, however, is not hers alone. It is the grief of
all those parents who cut off their children during life, only to
realize later their sad mistake.

WRITING ABOUT ESSAYS AND OTHER FORMS OF NONFICTION

The guidelines provided for writing about stories, poems, and plays can serve you for writing about essays and other forms of nonfiction as well. Your reasons for writing will often be similar to your reasons for writing about the other literary genres. The benefits are similar, too. And you can use the same types of informal writing strategies to get started—annotation, freewriting, and the double-column notebook.

Elements of Nonfiction

An essay or other work of nonfiction prose, like a work of fiction, poetry, or drama, can be studied from a number of perspectives. In addition to considering the work's literary, cultural, and historical contexts, we can also attend to its elements of style, structure, and thought.

Style.   Like poets, dramatists, and fiction writers, writers of nonfiction use language in literal and figurative ways. The kinds of figurative language most prevalent in essays are those that involve comparison, particularly in the forms of simile and metaphor. Writers of nonfiction use these forms of comparison to make one thing clear in terms of another. Sometimes the writer's intention in using the comparison is explicit, as when Francis Bacon, in pointing out the faults of young men, writes that a young man typically "will not acknowledge or retract them, like an unready horse that will neither stop nor turn." Bacon's comparison emphasizes their common quality of stubbornness.

On other occasions, writers employ more complex and less explicit comparisons, as when Bacon suggests that some men are not "ripe for action" until they reach middle age. The implicit comparison is between men and plants—specifically, fruit. Like fruit, men come to maturity over time.

In the same way that not all fruit ripens at the same time, not all men become ready for mature action at the same time. Some men, like some fruits, ripen faster than others.

Structure.   The structural features of nonfiction differ from those of novels and stories, poems and plays. Generally, nonfiction's structures involve a structure of thought, a series of organizational patterns that enable writers to develop ideas in forms both convenient and efficient. Depending on the nonfiction genre that writers employ, their organizational structures will vary. Autobiographers often employ the structure of chronology or time to organize their work. They also rely on the role memory plays in creating patterns of association that serve as structural devices, with one memory leading to another, even when the memories occur out of chronological order.

Historians also rely, to some extent, on chronology to order the details of their prose. Insofar as historians recount narrative stories about the past, they rely on chronological structure. Insofar as they explain causes and effects, actions and consequences, they may also use the before and after, the now and then of historical chronology to structure their discourse.

But they may also employ analytical structures, such as comparison and contrast, classification, and definition, to explain their ideas. These patterns of organization pervade nonfiction and serve to help writers elucidate their ideas in ways readers can readily grasp. Being able to recognize that a writer is classifying information, as Darwin does in his *The Origin of Species,* or comparing one group of people with another, as Montaigne does in "Of Cannibals," or defining terms, as Jean-Paul Sartre does in "Existentialism and Humanism," enables readers to better understand writers' ideas.

The major structural principle governing all forms of nonfiction, whatever specific forms a writer's organization might take, is the back-and-forth movement between idea and evidence, ideas and supporting details. In reading nonfiction prose, a reader's primary goal is to discern the writer's idea, the general point being made about a topic, and evaluate the evidence in the form of supporting detail the writer presents to persuade readers of its validity and value. A writer's supporting details may appear in the form of anecdotes or stories, examples, reasons, facts, statistics, allusions, and other references to authorities.

Thought.   When authors choose to write nonfiction rather than poetry, fiction, or drama, they have some idea they wish to communicate directly. The choice of factual rather than fictional discourse testifies to the nonfiction writer's concern for expressing an idea. Even when essayists, autobiographers, and historians rely on narrative to tell stories or on description to convey feelings and attitudes, their emphasis is most often on expressing an idea. It is this primacy of idea that distinguishes nonfiction from other forms of imaginative writing.

Even though writers may choose to express themselves in nonfiction prose, their ideas do not exist independently of expressed feelings and attitudes. The ideas we discover in nonfiction prose may be felt as much as they are thought out and thought through. They derive from writers' emotions as much as from their intellects. This is yet another way in which nonfiction prose shares common ground with the imaginative literary modes of fiction, poetry, and drama.

STEPS TO WRITING A LITERARY ANALYSIS

- Annotate the work.
- Freewrite about the work—its characters, language, subjects, issues, perspective.
- Outline its structure; identify its parts and their functions.
- Identify its speaker, narrator, characters, voices. Briefly explain the role or function of each, and identify their key relationships.
- Describe the setting of the work and what the time and place of its action contribute to its meaning.
- Consider its point of view (fiction), sound play (poetry), staging (drama), perspective (nonfiction).
- Discuss your observations and impressions of the work with a few classmates.
- Select two key passages from different parts of the work and explain why each is important. Relate the passages to each other.
- Write a draft of an essay in which you use your detailed observations, developed in the previous steps, as the basis for developing an interpretation of the work. See the guidelines for drafting an essay in Chapter 2.
- After receiving feedback from your instructor and your classmates on your draft, revise your essay. See the guidelines for revision, editing, and proofreading in Chapter 2.

THE
HUMANITIES

7
Writing
with Sources

Research writing is one of the most challenging kinds of writing you can do. It requires not only development of an idea, claim, or thesis, as in your other kinds of essay writing, but also use of primary or secondary sources, which you must integrate smoothly and naturally into your own writing. In addition, research writing adheres to strict rules of documentation and citation by which you indicate what sources of information you are using and precisely what you have taken from them.

In spite of, or perhaps because of, its complexity, research writing can be extremely rewarding. Doing research—gathering information from libraries, people, the Internet—can be exciting, as you learn about a subject through reading intensively about it. The challenge of putting together your findings in a research essay or report that reflects your perspective or point of view on what you have learned can bring great intellectual enjoyment.

One reason to do research about works of art is to understand them better. Another is to see how they have been interpreted in the past. Scholars who have devoted their lives to the study of particular artists, writers, architects, or composers can provide insights that can enrich your understanding and deepen your appreciation of the artworks you study.

THE RESEARCH ASSIGNMENT

Your instructor may assign you a specific research topic, a general topic that you have to narrow down in an acceptable way, or an open topic, which gives you the liberty to choose your own topic. Whatever kind of research assignment you are given, be sure that you understand its nature and requirements. Ask your instructor to clarify the purpose of the assignment.

Does your instructor expect you to write a three-page paper or one of a dozen pages—or something in between? Are you expected to type your paper, to use primary sources, secondary sources, or both? Are you being asked to focus on a single work using only one or two sources, on a single work using multiple sources, on multiple works and multiple sources? Are you expected to document your sources by providing footnotes or parenthetical citations and a bibliography or list of works cited? Be sure to clarify the specific requirements of the research writing assignment.

Because so much is often at stake in a research assignment—a heavy investment of time and work and perhaps a significant portion of a course grade—it is critical that you understand what you are supposed to do for the assignment. Asking questions early on can save you from wasting large amounts of time later. It can also prevent misunderstanding, reduce frustration, and generally improve your chances of producing a piece of researched writing that meets your instructor's expectations.

Selecting a Topic

Let's suppose you are asked to write a brief paper—say, five to seven typed pages, double-spaced, approximately 1250 to 1750 words. You need to cite a minimum of six sources, at least three of which must be from periodicals or the Internet and three from books. You also are required to prepare a bibliography or works cited list.

Instructors sometimes provide topics, either by assigning everyone the same topic (or some variation of it) or by giving individual students assigned topics of their own. If that is your situation, you can skip down to the next section on finding and using sources. Most often, however, you will need to choose your own topic for a research essay, paper, or report.

You can do a number of things to simplify the task of finding a topic. First, ask your instructor for suggestions. Second, look over your class notes and your reading notes for key points of emphasis, for repeating issues and concerns, and for provocative questions and complex ideas.

Third, talk with other students, with both your classmates and with students who have already written papers for the course you are now taking. Fourth, consult other sources with information about the artist, composer, author, and work (or works) you will be writing about. A general reference work on artists, composers, or authors will provide you with an overview of his or her life, works, and influence. Finally, you can get ideas for topics from the questions raised in Chapters 3 and 4.

Your aim in using these human and library resources is to develop a viable topic, one you can explore in the allotted number of pages required for the research assignment. It should be a topic you can say something thoughtful about, with some degree of detail and specificity. It's a good idea to clear your topic with your instructor. Your instructor can help you shape the topic, perhaps by narrowing or broadening it in ways that might make it more manageable, more sharply focused, and potentially more engaging.

Working with an Assigned Topic

If you are given a topic by your instructor, you may still have room to focus or narrow it. Suppose, for example, that for an English course, you are required to write a research essay on one of the writers you are studying. You have selected or been assigned to write on the American fiction writer Ernest Hemingway. But the assignment is no more specific than to "write a research essay on some facet of the author's work." Let's say that the paper is to be approximately 2,500 words—about ten typed pages, double-spaced. It must include at least eight sources, to which you refer with in-text parenthetical citations at some point in your essay. And it must include a "Works Cited" list which you present in proper format.

Your task is to read some work or works by Hemingway and some secondary sources about his writing. In the process, you are to come up with a narrowed topic, along with an idea, thesis, or claim about it. You are to write an essay that presents your idea, thesis, or claim along with the evidence to support it. This evidence will come from the text of the writer's work and from the secondary sources of information you consult. You can find these secondary sources in your library's books and journal articles. You can also find information on Hemingway through the Internet, and you can access the holdings of your school and other public and private university libraries through the Internet.

Let's consider first how to use a typical library to find information needed for a research project. We will follow with information on using the Internet and the World Wide Web.

Using a Library to Conduct Research

Knowing that information is accumulated and stored in the library, however, is not enough. You need to know how to access that information efficiently and effectively. Because a typical college or university library stores so much information, it may prove daunting for a new student to know where to begin to acquire the information he or she needs. Be aware, first of all, that the resources of your college or university library extend even beyond its holdings, however vast they may be. In this age of spectacular communications, libraries are able to communicate with one another and to share their resources to the ultimate benefit of all users.

One way to make the transition to acquaintance with your library is through its staff. Take the opportunity to speak with one or more members of your library staff. Ask them for their help in gaining familiarity with their (and your) library's resources. They will be only too happy to assist you. Another way to gain access to a large university library is to speak with more experienced students who have used the library's resources.

Finding Books. To find books in your college library, you need to know two things. First, you have to find out how to access the books. Second, you need to locate the books themselves.

Your books will be catalogued in a computerized catalog accessed through online database computerized technology. You can access books in these ways: by *title* (should you know it); by *author* (should you know the author's name); and by *subject* (should you be searching to see what books your library has on a particular subject).

Accessing Books Using the Library Catalog. The first thing you should know in using an online catalog is whether or not it is integrated. An *integrated catalog* combines the author, title, and subject cards in a single catalog system arranged alphabetically. The alternative filing system typically separates the index into two or three parts: one part for subjects, a second for authors and titles, and sometimes a third just for titles. The most common system, however, and the most efficient is the integrated catalog.

Here are sample listings from an integrated catalog:

Author Listing

```
PS 3515    Lawrence, Frank M. Hemingway and
           the Movies.
E37 Z689   Jackson: University Press of Mississippi.
           c 1981. xix, 329 p.: ill; 24 cm.
```

Title Listing

PS 3515   <u>Hemingway and the Movies</u>. Frank M.
              Lawrence.

E37 Z689   Jackson: University Press of
              Mississippi. c. 1981. xix, 329 p.: ill;
              24 cm.

Subject Listing

PS 3515   Hemingway, Ernest. <u>Hemingway and
              the Movies</u>.

E37 Z689   Frank M. Lawrence. Jackson: University
              Press of Mississippi. c 1981. xix, 329
              p. ill; 24 cm.

Notice that all are listings for the same book: *Hemingway and the Movies* by Frank M. Lawrence. The first listing, an author reference, will be found alphabetized according to the first letters of the author's last name. The second listing, by title, can be found alphabetized according to the words and letters of the book's title. And the third listing, by subject, is found similarly alphabetized in a section of the online catalog devoted to Ernest Hemingway as a subject. This and other subject listings for Hemingway (or any other writer, artist, or composer) will be found alphabetized according to the author's *last* name.

It is important, however, to distinguish Hemingway as a subject from Hemingway as an author. When you pop up "Hemingway" in the online catalog, you will find first listings for books that Ernest Hemingway wrote. His works will be listed alphabetically beginning with *Across the River and into the Trees* and ending with *Winner Take Nothing* (if your library has those books). Following the computer listings for books Hemingway wrote will be listings for books written *about* Hemingway. In this group of subject listings, also alphabetically arranged, you will find books such as *Hemingway and the Movies, The Hemingway Hero,* and *The Hemingway Women.*

Accessing Books Using an Online Database.   One of the first things you should ask is what the online system includes. Does it include all the books in your school library? only those acquired before or after a certain date? This is especially important for finding periodicals, magazines, journals, and newspapers published periodically—monthly, weekly, annually, and so on. You need to know both what is in the system and what is not.

Searching for Ernest Hemingway.   Let's say you want to look up Ernest Hemingway. You will need to indicate by a specific system command (punching the S key on your computer keyboard, for example) if you want to search for titles about Hemingway as a subject, including books in which the word *Hemingway* appears as part of the title. To search for Hemingway's works, you would punch another key (the A key perhaps) to tell the system you want to conduct a search for an author. Once you tell the system how to search, it will present you with a list of categories. Here, for example, is what part of one university library online catalog lists for Hemingway as author. The first eight and the last eight entries of the seventy-nine books included among the university's holdings are listed.

```
Hemingway, Ernest:

 1. 88 Poems
 2. Across the River and into the Trees
 3. Across the River and into the Trees
 4. By-line
 5. The Collected Stories
 6. Complete Short Stories
 7. Correspondence
 8. The Dangerous Summer
 . . . . . . . . . . . . . . . . . . . . .
72. The Sun Also Rises
73. Three Novels
74. To Have and Have Not
75. To Have and Have Not
76. To Have and Have Not
77. Winner Take Nothing
78. Winner Take Nothing
79. Winner Take Nothing
```

The repeated titles at numbers 2–3 and 77–79 reflect holdings among the university's different campus libraries.

Notice that, if the library has numerous books on a subject or by an author, it organizes these books into categories. So to begin to see actual titles on the screen, you need to perform one additional step. You need to look over the list of numbered categories, and then tell the computer which category to display. Suppose you wish to look up Hemingway as subject to see what has been written about him. Here is what could appear for Hemingway as subject in an online catalog:

```
1. Hemingway, Ernest 1898                            1 entry
2. Hemingway, Ernest 1899–1961                      52 entries
3. Hemingway, Ernest 1899–1961 Appreciation  1 entry
4. Hemingway, Ernest 1899–1961 Appreciation– 1 entry
                               Germany
5. Hemingway, Ernest 1899–1961 Bibliography 10 entries
6. Hemingway, Ernest 1899–1961 Biography    12 entries
7. Hemingway, Ernest 1899–1961 Juvenile      1 entry
                               letters
8. Hemingway, Ernest 1899–1961 Biography–    3 entries
                               Marriage
```

Notice that category 2 includes 52 entries. Because the category has no heading, to find out the kinds of books included within it, you would have to press 2 and scan through the listings. We will look at a shorter list, that for 8, Biography—Marriage. Here are the books that appear on the screen when you press 8:

```
1. Along with Youth: Hemingway: The Early Years
   Griffin, Peter
2. Hadley Diliberto, Gioia
3. The Hemingway Women, Dert, Bernise
4. How It Was, Hemingway, Mary Welsh
```

To view the information, including call numbers of these books, location, and other information, you would simply press the appropriate number. You will be given information about the length and size of the book, its publication data, and location. Most systems also provide information about the book's availability.

   In browsing in one of these books about Hemingway's marriages, you might get an idea for a research paper that focuses on the marriages depicted in one or more of Hemingway's novels or short stories. Reading the works in the context of biographical sources can be supplemented by reading other secondary sources that are less biographical than interpretive or analytical. And of course you should reread the primary sources—in this case, Hemingway's own writing.

Finding Periodical Articles.   You can locate articles in popular magazines and scholarly journals in any number of ways. First, you can find current issues of periodicals displayed in a special section, where you can peruse them in the library. Usually a handful of back issues of each periodical to which your library subscribes is available for casual reading and browsing.

If you need issues of magazines or journals that are more than a few months old, you will probably need to access those periodicals either by means of the computerized database or by using one or more of the periodical indexes. The basic procedure is the same.

Periodical indexes are organized by subject rather than by author or title. Periodical indexes cover a specific group of periodicals which are identified with their abbreviations at the front of the index or volume. The *Social Sciences Index* provides references to articles published in periodicals pertaining to sociology, psychology, political science, economics, and other social science subject categories. The *Humanities Index* refers you to articles about literature and history; music, art, and film; religion and philosophy; and other related subjects.

Because the vast majority of information in periodicals is not reprinted in books, it is important to learn how to use indexes to different subjects. Here are some important ones:

The *Art Index* is an index of articles and reviews about the arts, including not only painting, drawing, sculpture, and architecture, but also photography, decorative arts, city planning, and interior design—for non-Western as well as for Western civilizations.

The *Bibliography of the History of Art* covers the visual arts in all media but covers only Western art from late antiquity to the present.

Architectural Periodicals Index indexes about 500 journals. It is available online as *The Architecture Database* (DIALOG), with files since 1973.

The *Modern Language Association International Bibliography of Books and Articles in Modern Language and Literature* is a comprehensive index to literature and language arranged by national literatures and subdivided by literary periods.

The *Annual Bibliography of English Language and Literature* is a subject index of articles chronologically arranged.

The *Humanities Index,* formerly the *Social Sciences and Humanities Index,* covers a wide range of subjects, from archaeology to religion.

Historical Abstracts includes abstracts of scholarly articles on world history exclusive of the United States and Canada.

The *Philosopher's Index* includes scholarly articles and books and periodicals indexed by subject and author.

Religion Index One: Periodicals provides a subject and author index of scholarly articles on topics of religion published in Protestant, Catholic, and Jewish periodicals.

Interlibrary Loan.   You can request to borrow books and journal articles from other libraries via interlibrary loan. In order to do so, however, you must provide your librarian with precise information concerning the book or periodical. Titles and authors of books with call numbers will usually suffice. For periodical articles, provide the exact name of the periodical, its publication date and/or volume number, and the pages you need. This information, by the way, is critical at every stage of your access of periodical material. When you first copy the information from the periodical index, you must be careful to identify the periodical correctly, as well as to take down volume, date, and page numbers. Your librarian may need this to pick the right issue from closed stacks. Or you may need it to find the correct microfilm or bound volume and then the appropriate pages for reading. And finally, later, when it comes time to write your report or research paper, you will need this information for proper documentation.

THE ELECTRONIC LIBRARY

Although college and university libraries continue to hold printed copies of periodical indexes, much of your periodical and book searches will be conducted via computer and CD-ROM. The age of electronic information storage and retrieval has arrived, and it is critical that you learn to access your university's storehouse of information via electronic channels.

The most important guide to the new technology is your library staff, especially the reference librarians. To maximize results, you need to have specific questions for them. Let them know exactly what you are looking for, and why. Inform them about what you have already done, what you know, which equipment you are already familiar with. Then ask what else they might suggest. More than likely they will suggest a database you are unaware of or a piece of equipment you don't know the library owns. All you have to do is ask.

Once you begin following up on their suggestions, and once you have begun to use the new technology, don't hesitate to return for additional help. Chances are, the next time around you will ask a more specific question that can be addressed more quickly and efficiently than the first time you seek the reference librarians' assistance.

In addition to the reference librarians, you can also solicit the help of other students and faculty who are comfortable with using the latest technology. Most people will be more than happy to help you out. Don't expect them to conduct your searches; do, however, expect them to give you a few pointers. Finally, get your hands on your library's printed guidelines for use. These are invaluable, as they explain clearly and succinctly exactly what you need to know to use your library effectively.

USING THE INTERNET FOR RESEARCH

The vast computer network, the Internet, includes the World Wide Web (WWW or simply, "the Web"), a system of linked documents. Information is stored at sites on the Web, which are linked to other sites and which can be located by accessing the sites' web pages.

Gaining Access to the Internet

To gain access to the Internet you need a modem that connects your computer to a telephone or an internal interface card that links your computer with a mainframe computer that has a pathway to the Internet. You (or your university) also need an Internet service provider, with whom you (or your university) has an account so that you can use the system. If you haven't already done so, check with your computer services department or with your library staff (if you do not own your own computer).

Browsing the Web

To navigate your way around the Web, you point and click on underlined words and phrases on a given web site. Doing so enables you to move among electronic pathways, or hypertext links, among web pages and sites. When you move from link to link you are browsing the Web.

The very first screen you see at any WWW site is typically its home page. In fact, you may see the home page of the web browser software program (often either *Netscape Navigator* or *Internet Explorer*) you use to navigate or browse the WWW. These browsers employ search engines, another kind of software device, used to find information organized by categories. Among the most frequently used search engines are AltaVista, Webcrawler, and Yahoo.

Web browsers use the key words you enter on the home page (the topic for your search), select a search engine, and provide a list of sites that relate to the key words you selected. If after visiting the sites you haven't found the kind of useful information you need, you can change search engines, either by clicking a button for a particular search engine or by typing in its Internet address.

Some Dangers of Web based Research

Once you learn your way around the Web and can move about among sites, you will need some guidelines for selecting from the information you locate. You will need to decide which information is truly useful and which is not. And you will also need to evaluate the reliability of that information. Even more than with print sources, web sources often contain information that has not been carefully reviewed for accuracy. Because anyone can post information on the Web, you need to be especially careful that the sources provide current and accurate information. You can use the following guidelines to help you evaluate web sources:

Guidelines for Evaluating Web Sources

- Identify the individual or organization who established the source site.
- Consider how the source compares in care, thoroughness, accuracy, and currency with the print sources you have seen.
- Consider what special interest groups might think about the information from the source.
- Consider whether you think the source is good enough to cite in your research essay, paper, or report.

But how do you know if a source is reliable? One test is whether it has gone through a process of review, the way articles in scholarly journals and books published by reputable presses do. This is problematic for web sites, because they do not undergo a rigorous selection process. Among the most potentially untrustworthy sites are anonymous web sites, those whose origin and source you do not know.

Another question to ask yourself is whether the poster of the web site has a vested or special interest in the information the site includes. Check the information presented against other information gleaned from other web sites and from print sources.

And finally, consider how your audience might respond to the information on the web site should you use it as evidence or fact in your research essay, paper, or report.

USING SECONDARY SOURCES WISELY

For most topics you research you will find a multitude of sources—far more than you can read and use for your research assignment. From the start you will need to select from among them those most useful and relevant for your topic. In addition, you will need to evaluate the sources for credibility, reliability, and currency.

Avoid the temptation to begin reading thoroughly and taking notes from the first sources you find. Instead, compile a list of many sources—a dozen books and articles at least—before reading any of them carefully and before taking notes. Select your list of sources by looking carefully at titles and subtitles of books and articles. Look also at their dates of publication. Up-to-date information in journal articles may correct, supplement, or otherwise provide an advance on material published earlier in both journals and books.

Browse through your books and articles, skimming their tables of contents, indexes, and headings. Look to see how many pages are devoted to your topic. More often than not, you will find that in-depth treatment will be more useful for your research and writing than brief superficial coverage of your topic. Read the preface and introduction to books and the abstract or summary of articles, if available. These will give you a clearer sense of their relevance for your work than titles and tables of contents.

Once you begin reading your potential sources, read quickly at first, skimming through chapters and articles to gain a sense of their depth, degree of detail, level of difficulty, and general point of view. If you are researching a controversial subject, you should look for books and articles representing different points of view. You can determine an author's point of view by identifying his or her claims, kinds of evidence brought in their support, types of sources and authorities cited, and whether the author is affiliated with or represents a special interest group.

Regardless of your own point of view on an issue or topic, try to read with an open mind. Be careful to distinguish facts from emotional appeals.

Try also to question what you read; avoid simply accepting as truth every assertion you find.

You can use the following questions to analyze your sources:

- Does the title of the source provide a clue to its point of view? Does the title reveal bias?
- What is the author's professional affiliation and perspective on the topic?
- Does the evidence in the source seem persuasive?
- Does the author include opposing points of view?
- How well does the author support his or her argument and refute opposing views?
- What is the author's tone? How engaging are the author's ideas and arguments?

How can you use secondary sources without allowing them to dominate your research paper? The most important thing you can do is to read the literary work, look carefully at the work of art or architecture, listen repeatedly to the musical composition. In each encounter with the artwork, you should make and take notes, using the techniques described in Chapter 1. Through listing, annotating, freewriting, and reflecting on what you read, see, or hear, you can begin to form your own sense of the work.

Do the same thing when you read secondary sources. Photocopy them, if you can, so you can annotate them. Summarize the key claims made by the author of each source. Look for connections between the sources; identify contradictions and contrasting perspectives. Record in your notebook your own thinking about what the authors of the secondary sources say.

In addition, go back to the primary sources to read, look, or listen again. Jot down in your notebook new insights you have gained as a result of your reading in the secondary sources. Consider the extent to which you agree with what you have read in the secondary sources. You can use secondary sources you agree with to bolster an argument you wish to make about an artwork or to provide factual information about it. You can use a source you disagree with as a point of departure for your own views. If you agree in part with a source, you can make distinctions and express qualified agreement or approval in expressing your reservations as you develop your own perspective.

NOTE TAKING

When you are ready to take notes on your sources, be sure to list the complete bibliographical information from the source on an index card or on a list of sources you compile. List the author's name, the work's title and subtitle, place and date of publication. As you take notes, mark the exact pages you refer to for each of your notes. You will need accurate notes when you draft and document your paper. Taking care at this stage will save you time and aggravation later. Careful and accurate notes will also help you avoid plagiarism.

The notes you take will help you better understand the topic you are researching. They will also become evidence in support of the idea, thesis, or claim you develop in your research essay.

Try to make your notes more than a simple matter of copying from your sources or summarizing and paraphrasing their ideas and arguments. Use the note-taking stage of the research process to think and develop your ideas. Try to make connections among the ideas and evidence you find in your sources. Draw inferences and conclusions based on information they provide. Evaluate the inferences and conclusions they present.

You will also have to decide whether to write your notes on index cards or in a notebook or to use a computer. Whatever method you use, be sure to distinguish carefully between your words and ideas and those of your sources. If you think you may use a source extensively in your paper, you may wish to photocopy it.

Taking Efficient Notes

Among the problems a beginning researcher confronts is when to begin taking notes, how many notes to take, and what kind of notes to take. The solution to these note-taking problems is to consider the purpose of your research—your research question or topic and the thesis or claim you wish to make about it.

You should begin taking notes at the beginning of your research rather than reading through many sources before beginning your note taking. You may be tempted, however, as you begin doing research, to take down too much. It is more useful, however, and more efficient, to write down less rather than more at the early stages.

To be selective, you should try to imagine how a given source might be used in your paper. Will the information and ideas be used to provide background information? Will they be used as part of an analysis of a problem or issue? Will they be used to illustrate different approaches or points of view? Will they be used to provide evidence in support of your position or claim? Will they be used as part of a counterview, which you will argue against?

Considering such questions about the information, ideas, and views presented in a source can help you not only in deciding what you need to extract from it, but also in how your own thinking can enrich, support, qualify, or refute it. Introducing your own reflections into your note taking is extremely important for at least two reasons: (1) it helps you avoid being swayed by every different source you read; (2) it helps you develop and refine your thinking about your research topic so that the final product becomes "yours" and not just a compilation of the views of others.

In general your purposes in note taking will be to gather data and information or to understand varying perspectives or points of view. If the purpose of your research project is informative or explanatory, you note the kinds of notes that gather, select, and organize the information that appears germane and interesting to your prospective audience. If your purpose is analytical and interpretive, you look for patterns and connections in the sources' information and ideas, so that you can provide an interesting way to understand the issue, text, or problem you are analyzing and interpreting. If your purpose is persuasive, you look at the information and ideas in your sources as potential evidence to support your claim about the topic. Along the way, whichever your purpose, you will need to accurately summarize and paraphrase the ideas and perspectives you find, whether you agree with them initially or not.

Summarizing and Paraphrasing Secondary Sources

Note taking requires summarizing and paraphrasing sources. When you summarize, you condense the material in your source and put it into your own words and sentences. A summary is always shorter than the original—sometimes considerably shorter. It captures the author's main idea so that other readers can readily understand it.

In summarizing, try to represent an author's point of view fairly and to present his or her ideas accurately. When you paraphrase, you recast an author's words into your own language, translating pretty much sentence for sentence the author's idea and supporting evidence. A paraphrase, which is approximately the same length as the original source, follows its structure and includes more details than a summary. When summarizing and paraphrasing, be especially careful to use your own language—your own words. If you find yourself using the words and sentences of your source, you will have to use quotation marks to indicate that. (For more on summarizing and paraphrasing, see Chapter 1.)

Quoting

You should quote from a source only when the language of the source is especially striking or memorable, or when the quotation will strengthen your argument because the source is an important authority on the topic. You might also decide to quote a source if you wish to argue against the author or when you want an author's exact words to express the outrageousness of a claim or the weakness of an argument.

When you quote, be sure to quote the writer's words exactly and to put quotation marks around them. To indicate that the source contains an error, add the Latin word *sic* (meaning "thus") in brackets immediately following the error. For example, "Franklin Delano Rosevelt [*sic*] created the memorable phrase 'The New Deal.'"

When you want to emphasize a few words of a quotation, underline or italicize them, but be sure to indicate that the emphasis is yours by adding the words "my emphasis." For example, in a recent article in the *New York Times,* the German government was reported to have "revalued its gold reserves in an effort to comply with the economic conditions necessary for ensuring readiness for the establishment of a common European currency. The German revaluation, however, is an accounting trick the German government has *hypocritically condemned* for other countries," such as Italy and Spain (my emphasis).

To indicate that something has been omitted from an occasion, use *ellipses*—three spaced periods (. . .). Writers shorten long quotations with ellipses; they also use ellipses when only certain parts of the quotation are relevant to their discussion. You could shorten the previous example about Germany's revaluation of its gold reserves by using ellipses: Germany "revalued its gold reserves . . . an accounting trick" that many have seen as hypocritical after Germany condemned the same practice by other countries.

Integrating Quotations

Depending on length, you might integrate a quotation into your text by embedding it in quotation marks or setting it off from your text without quotation marks. Incorporate brief quotations (fewer than four typed lines

[MLA] or 40 words [APA] for prose, and three lines for poetry), directly
into the text of your paper.

```
Johnson claims "The judiciary, not the executive
branch of government, is most seriously in need
of reform today" (156).
```

```
"The judiciary," Johnson claims, "not the
executive branch of government, is most seriously
in need of reform today" (156).
```

If you wish to weave a sentence—or a part of it—into your own sentence, you might do it like this:

```
It is not the executive branch of government,
Johnson claims, but the judiciary that "is most
seriously in need of reform today" (156).
```

```
Johnson claims that it is not the executive branch
of government that needs reform. He suggests,
rather, that it is the judiciary that "is most
seriously in need of reform today" (156).
```

For longer quotations, indent the passage ten spaces or one inch
rather than five spaces or one-half inch. Double-space and do not use quotation marks. Depending on the context, you may use a colon (:) to introduce a block quotation:

```
Johnson's argument differs from Whelan's. Here is
how Johnson sees the issue:
```

```
It is not the executive branch of government but
the judiciary that is most seriously in need of
reform today. Moreover, if judicial abuses are
not stopped and immediately corrected, both
business investment and the general quality of
life in the country will plummet. (156)
```

Occasionally you may need to modify a quotation slightly by altering one of its words or by adding a word so that the quotation fits the grammatical structure of your sentence.

```
Without adequate judicial reform, Johnson
envisions "both business and the general quality
of life in the country . . . plummet[ing]" (156).
```

The ellipsis (. . .) indicates that one or more words have been omitted from the sentence (in this case, "will"). Notice that the changed word contains brackets [ ] around the part not included in the original quotation.

Plagiarism

Avoid *plagiarism*—that is, using someone else's words, ideas, or organizational patterns in writing without crediting the source. Writers sometimes fail to acknowledge their sources properly, resulting in plagiarism, a kind of verbal kidnapping or theft. Some writers—especially student writers—believe that plagiarism occurs only when an author's exact words are used without acknowledgment. But this is only one type of plagiarism.

Plagiarism also involves borrowing or using the ideas or structure of argument of an author without acknowledging your source. Even when you use your own words to summarize or paraphrase the words and ideas of a source, you must acknowledge your source. If you do not, you have plagiarized another's work and presented it as your own.

Some students plagiarize out of ignorance; others, out of fear. Some believe that they must only record references to exact and direct quotations, but this, as we have indicated, is not true. Others think that if they document all the ideas they have borrowed from others, there will be nothing left of "them" in their research writing. So they plagiarize out of fear that they have nothing to say of their own.

Still others plagiarize because when they read sources—of art or literary criticism, of cultural analysis, of historical description—they find the writing so clear and the arguments so cogent that they cannot think of ways to convert their source's information and style of writing into their own. So they copy without quoting.

Although it is normal to experience some anxiety when writing a research paper, essay, or report, do not give in to the temptation to plagiarize. Instead, spend more time reading, writing, and thinking. Become more and more familiar with the ideas and issues you are writing about. Talk about them with classmates, friends, and instructors. Then plunge in, for better or worse, with your own ideas presented in your own words.

Here is an example of how a passage from a source can be plagiarized and also paraphrased without plagiarism:

Original source

Two genetically identical twins inside a womb will unfold in slightly different ways. The shape of the kidneys or the curve of the skull won't be quite the same. The differences are small enough that an organ from one twin can probably be transplanted into the other. But with the organ called the brain, the differences become profound. George Johnson, "Don't Worry. A Brain Still Can't Be Cloned," New York Times, 2 March 1997.

Plagiarism

In a recent article George Johnson notes that two genetically identical twins inside a womb will unfold in slightly different ways.

Comment: This is plagiarism because the words "two . . . ways." should be placed in quotation marks, as they are George Johnson's words.

Plagiarism

Cloning is not as sure a thing as some people believe largely because the development of the human brain differs in profound ways from the way other bodily organs develop.

Comment: This is plagiarism because there is no acknowledgment that the idea here came from George Johnson's article.

Plagiarism

Genetically identical twins unfold in the womb in similar but slightly different ways. And although the differences are small enough so that organs from one twin can be transplanted into the other, the shape of a kidney or curve of the head won't be exactly the same.

Comment: Here the writer is mixing his own words with phrases of the source. It's as if the plagiarizing writer is trying to hide the fact of his near-copying of the source by changing a word or phrase here and there.

Acceptable Paraphrase

```
George Johnson suggests that human cloning is
not as close to becoming a reality as some might
think. This is so, according to Johnson, pri-
marily because of the development of the human
brain, which differs in its very complexity of
development from the simpler, more predictable
development of other bodily organs (15).
```

You can use the following guidelines for help in avoiding plagiarism:

Guidelines for Avoiding Plagiarism

- Allow ample time for writing papers, essays, and reports.
- Take notes on sources after you have read and understood a chapter or section, even a few paragraphs.
- Take notes in your own words as much as you can. Close the book or look away from your source so you can compose sentences and paragraphs that capture its gist or essence.
- Always distinguish clearly between your own words and those of a source, by putting quotation marks around what you copy from the source.
- Copy the author's name and page number beside each note you take; that is, alongside each idea or phrase you borrow from the source.
- Think when you take notes; that is, consider the persuasiveness or value of the source's comments and ideas. One way to do this is to draw a line under or next to the source's language or idea, so that you can then write out a couple of sentences about your reaction to the source.
- Avoid borrowing other students' papers or notes. Work only from your own notes on the sources you have read.
- Be sure to back up on a diskette not only your final draft, but earlier drafts and any notes you took on a computer. Save handwritten notes.

WRITING THE PAPER

In writing your research essay, paper, or report, follow the guidelines for drafting and revising provided in Chapter 1. Set aside sufficient time to work out the basic argument of your paper. This will involve the time necessary for tracking down sources, taking notes, and reflecting on their significance. Try, in your preliminary draft, to articulate your ideas without using your sources—or only using them slightly. Get your ideas down as clearly and fully as you can. Provide the evidence you need to sustain your argument or support your views by analyzing, interpreting, or evaluating the artwork itself that you are writing about. Then write a second draft in which you incorporate the relevant secondary sources.

Leave time for a third draft in which you further refine your thinking, taking into consideration additional evidence you find in the work itself or among the secondary sources. Use this third draft also to provide precise documentation for your sources.

In general, approach the drafting and revising of a research essay, paper, or report just as you would any other nonresearched assignment. Be careful to avoid letting your sources take over your paper.

Sample Research Papers

The following research papers provide samples of writing about a single work of art using sources, and writing about multiple works by one author. In the first research paper, Michael DiYanni analyzes Thomas Eakins's painting *John Biglin in a Single Scull* in the context of other of Eakins's rowing pictures. Michael used eleven sources for his research, although five of those sources were articles collected in a single volume, *Thomas Eakins: The Rowing Pictures*.

In the second research paper, Karen Elizabeth describes the importance of the father-son relationship in the work of the Czech writer Franz Kafka. Karen's well-organized paper explores this theme in three major works, which she takes up one after the other.

Michael DiYanni

Humanities 112

Professor Permut

December 1, 1998

Thomas Eakins's <u>John Biglin in a Single Scull</u>

"Rowing--the noblest, manliest, and approaching to the scientific, of any game, or sport, or play, in any nation, clime or country.

Robert B. Johnson

Thomas Eakins, <u>John Big-lin in a Single Scull,</u> 1874. Oil. 24⁵⁄₁₆ × 16″. Yale University Art Gallery.

By the time Thomas Eakins began serious study of art at the Pennsylvania Academy of Fine Arts in 1862, portraiture was no longer <u>en vogue</u> with American artists, as landscape and genre paintings had surpassed them in popularity. Photographs had also begun to supplant painting in the arena of portraiture. Despite its unpopularity, Eakins quickly decided that depicting through portraits the people around him was his true vocation, and he did so with directness and psychological penetration. Of the more than two hundred sitters and subjects Eakins depicted during his career, no more than twenty-five of his portraits were commissioned.[1] The artist himself sought out subjects, often friends, and looked for intimacy in his work.

Eakins's work was marked with a sense of "brutal realism,"[2] which did not seek to beautify or gloss over his subjects, but rather to arrive at their essential truth by depicting them realistically, in natural settings. Eakins was of a scientific mind, and his work shows a painstaking approach to exactness in lighting and perspective, along with an uncommon knowledge of anatomy and physiology.

Upon his return from study in Paris in 1870, the twenty-six-year-old Eakins entered an intense period of creativity. Now a professional painter, Eakins chose rowers as his primary subject for more than three years. Rowing was a natural choice of subject for Eakins, who was an accomplished oarsman, and who lived only a few short blocks from the Schuylkill River. The artist saw in rowing a sense of discipline and a combination of mental and physical virtue. Eakins was also a careful student of the human body, and paintings of rowers allowed him an opportunity to depict the body in action and motion. This gave him a chance to showcase his substantial physiological knowledge.

John Biglin in a Single Scull

Eakins found inspiration in John and Bernard (Barney) Biglin, two celebrated professional oarsmen from New York. The Biglin brothers had achieved a mastery of both types of rowing, "sweeps" (where each rower pulls one long oar that extends out to one side of the boat, or shell), and "sculls" (in which each oarsman pulls two oars, one in each hand). They were well matched: John at twenty-eight stood 5'9 and 3/4" and weighed 161 pounds; Barney, thirty-one, stood 5'9 and 1/2" and weighed 151 pounds. Both were universally respected for their skill and strength.[3]

John was considered a model of ideal rowing physique, "as besides being skillful and experienced in the art, he [was] endowed with great strength, presenting in appearance the perfect picture of an athlete."[4] He had developed his physique, working variously as a mechanic, laborer, foreman, fireman, and boatman. Barney was involved in predominantly mental work, having won in 1872 the first of several terms in the New York State Assembly.[5]

Thomas Eakins carved out for himself a unique place in the history of American art as a painter who could portray the individual as never before. His 1873 oil on canvas, <u>John Biglin in a Single Scull</u>, is a fine example of what set Eakins apart. It demonstrates his attention to lighting, perspective, and detail, coupled with a sense of forthrightness and intimacy that draws viewers into the world of the solitary sculler.

Perhaps Eakins's favorite subjects were members of the Biglin Crew. Anchored by brothers John and Barney Biglin, it was the best rowing outfit in the world. After numerous sketches, studies, and paintings of the Biglins in action, in which the young artist explored many facets of rowing, the mature artist Eakins painted a startling portrait of John racing in his single scull.

Eakins's oil on canvas, <u>John Biglin in a Single Scull</u>, was in fact a study made in preparation for a watercolor that Eakins had sent to his former mentor Gerome in 1874. The oil stands alone, however, with its photographlike cropping and the intimacy brought to the subject, giving it a sense of monumentality and an iconic power. Watercolor had become the artist's medium of choice for a short period in the mid-1870s. It was a difficult medium to work with, and Eakins first painted the oil (a much more forgiving medium, thanks to the slower time for the paint, and the ability to retouch and layer). The fact that Eakins put so much effort into this oil study is indicative of his methodical and painstaking approach to painting and his respect for and desire to please Gerome. Even before preparing the oil, Eakins drew a perspective sketch as a study almost twice the size of the finished watercolor. In his perspective studies for the work, Eakins noted the measured dimensions and coordinates for the reflections. He was aware of the exact measurements of his subjects, "a practice considered unnecessary by most American teachers of artistic perspective, who trained the eye to judge distances proportionally."[6] However, the precision that Eakins achieved was so great as to present scrupulous viewers with the ability to ascertain the time of day, and even the viewing position of Eakins himself from the paintings.

Once Eakins had completed the perspective sketches, he painted the oil on canvas. The image of Biglin is substantially larger that that of the watercolor, so that Eakins could prepare every detail before scaling the images down. It is seemingly a study for the figure of John Biglin himself, as less attention is paid to the background. Sailboats and an eight-oared shell seen near the horizon in both the perspective study and the watercolor are omitted in the oil painting. Eakins still concentrates on the reflection in the foreground, yet he gives less attention to the water in the background, which is glimmering with the summer sun in the watercolor. Instead, in the oil painting, Eakins leaves it an almost solid and cool blue. The cloudless sky, the shoreline, and the horizon all seem perfunctory.

It is the form of Biglin himself, poised near the start of his stroke that Eakins, instead, concentrates on. The champion oarsman is in perfect position, his body relaxed yet prepared to attack his next stroke. Biglin's wrists are firmly locked, and his left arm meets the oar at an acute angle, redirecting the oar's diagonal thrust toward his chest. These angles appear everywhere in the painting: the sharp angular meeting of the oar and the arm, the acute angle at which the rower's calf meets his thigh, and the meeting of the shell's rigger and oarlock. "Visually, Biglin seems but one part of the machine that he propels."[7]

The precision with which Eakins prepared his canvases can be illuminated thanks to x-ray and microscopic analysis. These technologies evidence careful etching and inking of certain outlines and perspective lines. The analysis also reveals much about Eakins's layering of paint. There is evidenace that the sky of the oil painting was reworked. Eakins may have "regarded a bright blue sky as distraction,"[8] as has been suggested. This reworking probably accounts for the later date, 1874, on a study for a watercolor completed in 1873. Close analysis reveals that Eakins composed the sky out of three distinct layers of blue paint, from bottom to top: "an intense medium blue, a light blue, and a muddy color applied with a palette knife."[9] This calmer, cooler blue contrasts the reds of Biglin's bandanna and crew top, which allow the oarsman to stand out.

It is the simplicity of this study, however, that allows the viewer to concentrate on Biglin. Here we see a portraitist focusing almost exclusively on his subject. Eakins paints John Biglin in the same manner that he is depicted in other of his works, staring stoically forward in perfect concentration. In many ways Eakins's oil study is a more powerful work than the watercolor it preceded. Cropping the spanning landscape gives the painting a sense of intimacy and mentality. Although it may lack the shimmering and airy qualities of the watercolor, the oil painting seems much more substantial in comparison.

The consistent colors and the larger size of Biglin convey a sense of solidity.

With his focus solely on the oarsman, Eakins imparts to his viewer a sense of the solitude of the single sculler. All that is visible in the background is the bow of a boat, indicating that a race is in progress. The legendary Biglin is in full command of the race, with almost a full boat-length lead. Despite the undoubtedly heated action, the painting has a static and immobile feel to it. This emphasizes the relaxation and control of the oarsman. The work has a concentrated power, a sense of honesty that make it an iconic painting of its subject.

John Biglin in a Single Scull shows Thomas Eakins at his best. In it we see the artist's love for portraiture, his precision and attention to detail, and his power to inhabit and convey his subjects. The painting stands as one of Eakins's greatest works; it is a precursor to The Gross Clinic and other Eakins portraits that have become classics of realism. It reveals not only much about John Biglin, but much also about Eakins himself--what he valued, how he painted, and where he was heading, artistically, at this point in his career. It is truly a portrait of an artist.

Notes

1 Elizabeth Johns, Thomas Eakins (Princeton: Princeton UP, 1983), p. xix.

2 Louise Gardner, Art Through the Ages, 10th ed. (Fort Worth: Harcourt Brace, 1996), p. 969.

3 Helen A. Cooper, ed., Thomas Eakins: The Rowing Pictures, (New Haven: Yale UP, 1996), p. 39.

4 Ibid.

5 Martin A. Berger, "Painting Victorian Manhood," in Thomas Eakins: The Rowing Pictures (New Haven: Yale UP, 1996), p. 116.

6 Amy B. Werbel, "Perspective in Thomas Eakins' Rowing Pictures," in Helen A. Cooper, ed., Thomas Eakins: The Rowing Pictures (New Haven: Yale UP, 1996), p. 85.

7 Berger, p. 116.

8 Christina Currie, "Thomas Eakins Under the Microscope: A Technical Study of the Rowing Paintings," in Helen A. Cooper, ed. Thomas Eakins: The Rowing Pictures (New Haven: Yale UP, 1996), p. 100.

9 Ibid.

Franz Kafka and the Fear of the Father

By Karen Elizabeth

Literature and Humanities 101

Mrs. Fehrs

March 30, 1997

Franz Kafka is generally considered to be one of the greatest writers of the twentieth century. His fictional works have been read and interpreted, analyzed and debated from the time of their publication early in the twentieth century. Some interpreters have emphasized the religious aspect of Kafka's novels and stories (Spann 59). Others have claimed that his fiction should be interpreted from the standpoint of Freudian psychoanalysis (Greenberg 47). While these approaches are certainly interesting, it seems more natural to consider Kafka's fiction as reflecting his life, especially his relations with his father. Many of Kafka's fictional works, in fact, describe a conflict between an authoritative father (or father-figure) and a weak son, a conflict so powerful as to make the son feel tremendous guilt under the father's authoritative accusations. Among Kafka's fiction, "The Judgment," "The Metamorphosis," and <u>The Trial</u> illustrate how an all-powerful father or father-figure nearly destroys a weak and helpless dependent son.

Although Franz Kafka never married, he nonetheless carried on an intensive correspondence with a number of different women with whom he was engaged. These letters along with a long and complex letter to his father (a letter he never sent) reveal Kafka's fears and anxieties. They also indicate how intensely devoted he was to the craft of writing fiction.

One of Kafka's earliest stories, "The Judgment," was written in a single sitting. Kafka began the story at ten o'clock on the night of September 22, 1912 and finished it at six A.M. the next morning (Hayman 1). "The Judgment" recounts the story of Georg Bendemann, who has written to a friend in Russia about his impending engagement to be married. Before sending the letter, however, he feels the need to secure his father's approval, and thus enters his room to tell him about the letter. The father's reaction is very strange. He accuses his son of not telling him the whole truth about his friend. At one point, in fact, he even suggests that his son does not really have this friend in Russia at all. Later, he indicates that he does believe Georg has such a friend, but he is not in Russia. More importantly, however, in both cases, Georg's father believes that his son has lied to him.

Following these surprising and confusing (for Georg) accusations come two other criticisms. First, Georg's father accuses him of not being a very good businessman. (Georg works with his father in their family business.) The father accuses Georg of closing deals and getting credit that he doesn't really deserve, since his father arranges everything except the final details. Even more disturbing to Georg is his father's suggestion that he has not been a very good son, that his friend would have been a much better son to him than Georg. The father follows this cruel comment with words and actions that attempt to put the son in his place--subordinate to him. He tells Georg that he is not ready to be replaced in the business by his son, that he is indeed stronger than his son, that in attempting to deceive his father and overcome his authority, Georg deserves punishment. He then sentences him to death by drowning, and in the strangest of this story's series of bizarre occurrances, Georg leaves the house and jumps off a bridge to do exactly what his father orders (Heller 54-66).

"The Judgment" can be explained as a reflection of Franz Kafka's life at the time it was written. It is important for describing the "deeply disturbed father-son relation . . . in Kafka's life" (Spann 55). Kafka himself described this relationship thoroughly in his "Letter to His Father," in which he explains and defends himself against all his father's accusations while criticizing and blaming his father for terrifying him as a child and a young man (Heller 186-236). In this letter Kafka writes to his father that he would like "a diminution of your unceasing reproaches." He describes these reproaches as "a judgment of me." He comments that "as a father you have been too strong for me" ("Letter" 186-187). And he sums up by explaining that what was "incomprehensible" to him was "the suffering and shame you could inflict . . . with your words and judgments" ("Letter" 194).

II

The struggle of father with son, the powerful authority that the father exercises over his son, and the death of the son in "The Judgment" are central features of "The Metamorphosis" as well. As

Martin Greenberg points out, the "story is about death. . . . The first sentence . . . announces Gregor Samsa's death and the rest of the story is his slow dying" (Greenberg 70).

Why Gregor dies is one of the important questions of the story. One answer is that he dies of neglect and loneliness. In the same way that Gregor's father had mistreated and humiliated him, Gregor's mother and sister eventually come to abandon him. Although they had initially sympathized with his metamorphosis, before long they tire of it. They no longer think of the giant insect as their son and brother, and they leave him alone to die. Gregor Samsa, like Georg Bendemann of "The Judgment" and like Kafka himself, is a lonely person. Many details of "The Metamorphosis," from Gregor's being locked in his room to his inability to communicate with his family, to his being misunderstood by his boss, to his memories of his days before the metamorphosis, all indicate how alone he was.

Kafka himself was lonely and alienated from the society he lived in. He was a German-speaking Jew living in Prague, Czechoslovakia, where anti-German and anti-Semitic feelings were strong (Spann 17-20). And as he himself indicates repeatedly in "Letter to His Father," Kafka felt alienated from his family, especially from his father. This loneliness, however, was a consequence of his sense of inferiority, of being insignificant and unimportant. Perhaps that is one reason that when Kafka wrote "The Metamorphosis," he transformed Gregor Samsa into an insect, something normally regarded as insignificant.

Some of the most compelling and memorable scenes of "The Metamorphosis" are those in which Gregor's father interacts with him. In the first part of the story, when Gregor's father first realizes his son's metamorphosis, he "knotted his fist with a fierce expression on his face as if he meant to knock Gregor back into his room" (Heller 13). A bit later, his father "pitilessly" drives him back into the room, "hissing and crying 'Shoo', like a savage" ("Metamorphosis" 16). And finally, at the end of the first part of the story, when Gregor gets stuck trying to get back into his room, his father gives him a hard shove.

These actions, however, are only preliminaries. In the second and third parts of the story, Gregor's father behaves in an even more menacing fashion. Gregor is afraid at one point that his father will try to step on him as Kafka describes how "Gregor was dumbfounded at the enormous size of his [father's] shoe soles. Gregor, as Kafka writes, "could not risk standing up to him, aware . . . that his father believed only the severest measures suitable for dealing with him" (33). One of these severe measures is taken when Gregor's father bombards him with apples, lodging one in Gregor's back. Later, the wound from this apple begins to fester, and very likely contributes to Gregor's eventual death.

Kafka's real-life relations with his father, especially his feelings of inferiority, explain much of what happens in the fictional "The Metamorphosis." Gregor Samsa's inability to speak understandably, for example, may be related to Kafka's complaint that his father hardly ever let him talk. In his letter, Kafka blames his father for his temporarily losing the "capacity to talk." "At a very early age," he writes in the letter, "you forbade me to speak, silencing the oppositional forces that were disagreeable to you" (Heller 195).

But even more powerful and frightening was the feeling of guilt that Kafka's father made him experience. Something of this guilt is shown in "The Judgment." Perhaps that is why Georg Bendemann really kills himself. He believes the accusation that his father makes against him. Something of this guilt is also apparent in "The Metamorphosis." Perhaps that is one of the reasons Gregor remains a lonely bachelor taking care of his aging parents before his metamorphosis. He may have felt guilty about leaving them alone. And so, like Franz Kafka himself, Gregor Samsa does not marry.

III

The most impressive and sustained expression of the guilt Kafka felt is reflected in his novel, <u>The Trial</u>. That work describes how Joseph K., the central character, one day receives an Inspector and two guards who announce that he has been accused of a crime and is to be arrested. What's interesting is that the crime is never identified. The first sentence of the book indicates that he has done nothing wrong. All through the book the reader never discovers what Joseph K. is accused of. Neither does Joseph K. Even stranger, however, than this lack of an identifiable offense, Joseph K. comes to believe that he is guilty of whatever it is he stands accused of. His problem is that he allows the allegations to damage him because he comes to accept them. The entire novel is based on K.'s gradual realization that it does not matter whether or not he committed the offense he is charged with. He is guilty anyway. This he believes and comes to accept as right and just.

The feeling that "one was already punished before one even knew that one had done something bad" was something Kafka had experienced repeatedly in his relations with his father ("Letter" 199). Throughout the "Letter to His Father" Kafka recounts instances of why he so often experienced "an increase in the sense of guilt" ("Letter 203). In fact, at one point Kafka describes his relationship with his father as one of being on trial, sometimes for things he had not known he had done. He describes the experience in fact as "this fearful trial . . . in which you still go on claiming to be judge" ("Letter" 224).

The human relationships of <u>The Trial</u> are complicated further by references Kafka makes to the work regarding his love life. Kafka was engaged to be married on more than one occasion. In each instance, Kafka broke off the engagement, partly because he felt that he should be married to his writing only, that he should devote himself completely to his work (Hayman 183-188). When Kafka's engagements "made him realize that marriage threatened his dream world, he was horrified and overcome with feelings of guilt" (Spann 90). But he also seemed to feel that he was not prepared for marriage. He felt, as he expressed it, "mentally incapable of marrying" ("Letter" 230). In addition, however, Kafka felt that marriage was barred to him because it was the domain of his father and thus was prohibited to him ("Letter" 230). Nonetheless, according to a number of critics, Kafka felt guilty about not marrying and raising a family, which he described as "the utmost a human being can succeed in doing" (Spann 106). At least one critic interprets Joseph K.'s punishment in <u>The Trial</u> as a fair punishment for the ineffectual and unworthy life K. has led up till the time of his arrest (Greenberg 114). Joseph K. is punished then because he has misused his life, because he has wasted time and opportunities. This is what Kafka himself meant as he often considered both his marriageless life and his writing.

Franz Kafka's works are interesting for how they reveal the complicated workings of the mind. It is not always clear what is happening to the characters or why it is happening. The action of these fictional works seems often like a bad dream. Things are happening that the main character has no ability to control. But as the critics suggest, this is because Kafka's works reveal the psychological state of mind of the central characters. They reveal their fear, their anxiety,

and their guilt. We can understand these works because, like the author
and the characters he creates, we too experience our own fears and
anxieties. We too sometimes question ourselves, condemn ourselves, and
put ourselves on trial.

Works Cited

Greenberg, Martin. <u>Kafka: The Terror of Art</u>. New York: Horizon Press,
    1965.

Hayman, Ronald. <u>Kafka: A Biography</u>. New York: Oxford University Press,
    1982.

Heller, Erich, ed. <u>The Basic Kafka</u>. New York: Simon and Schuster, 1979.

Kafka, Franz, "The Metamorphosis," in <u>Classics of Modern Fiction</u>, 4th
    edition. Ed. Irving Howe, New York: Harcourt, 1985.

Kafka, Franz. "The Judgment" and "Letter to His Father." <u>The Basic
Kafka</u>.
    Ed. Erich Heller. New York: Simon and Schuster, 1979.

Kafka, Franz. <u>The Trial</u>. New York: Schocken Books, 1937.

Spann, Meno. <u>Franz Kafka</u>. Boston: G.K. Hall, 1976.

WRITING ABOUT

THE
HUMANITIES

8
Documenting
Sources

In research essays and papers it is necessary to document sources—that is, to indicate where you obtain information, data, and ideas included in your work. Documenting your sources provides readers with a trail to follow should they wish to find additional information or should they wish to check the accuracy or justness of your use of your sources. Indicating what you have borrowed from sources also enables your readers to see what your own contribution to the discussion is. And, finally, documenting your sources lets your readers see the amount and quality of research you have used in developing your essay or paper.

IN-TEXT CITATIONS

When you cite or indicate a source used in your paper, you do so in the text just after the material requiring documentation. To simplify what was once a cumbersome system of footnotes, endnotes, and superscripts, the Modern Language Association (MLA) and the American Psychological Association (APA) have developed their own systems of in-text citations. We explain here the MLA system.

To cite sources using the MLA system, place the author's name and the page references in parentheses immediately following the material being documented. If the author's name has been given in the text of your writing, provide only the page number in parentheses following the cited material.

Here is an example of each:

Author not named:
```
The evolution of the human
species has been a hotly
debated issue since the time of
Charles Darwin (Hugo 12).
```

Author named:
```
As Michael Hugo has pointed
out, the evolution of the
human species has been a hotly
debated issue since the time
of Charles Darwin (12).
```

Notice that, in both examples, the period comes after the parenthetical page citations.

In the event that you wish or need to cite a quotation from a source quoted in the source you are actually using, use the following model as an example. Suppose, for example, that you found the Hugo quotation shown earlier, not in the original source, but in another source you were reading, let's say in a book entitled *The Origins of Humankind* by Sheryl Fulton.

Here is what you would do to indicate that kind of borrowing:

```
"The debate over humanity's origins has been
going on ever since Darwin's The Descent of Man"
(qtd. in Fulton 21).
```

LISTING SOURCES AT THE END

In addition to the in-text citations for documenting sources within a research essay or paper, you must also provide, at the end of your paper, a list of the sources you cite within it. That list of sources is a Bibliography or Works Cited, which includes more detailed bibliographical information than the brief in-text parenthetical citations described earlier.

ʌs are listed alphabetically by authors' last names. The first line ʌtry is placed flush against the left margin, with subsequent lines indenteʌ five spaces.

```
Author. Title. City of Publication: Publisher,
     year of publication.

Karnow, Stanley. In Our Image: America's Empire
     in the Philippines. New York: Random, 1989.
```

Before providing examples of the various formats for books—with multiple, anonymous, and corporate authors, with editors, in multiple volumes, translations, special series and editions—and formats for articles in a similarly dizzying array of variations, we explain briefly how to cite sources using the footnote/endnote format.

Sometimes referred to as CMS style (for its source, the *Chicago Manual of Style*), footnote/endnote format features in-text numbered note references linked to endnotes describing works cited, plus a bibliography for full reference details.

Notes

Endnotes are placed together at the end of a paper; footnotes are placed at the bottom (or foot) of individual pages of a paper. Like the MLA in-text parenthetical citations, footnotes and endnotes provide publication information about sources you quote, paraphrase, summarize, or otherwise reference in the text of your paper. Place superscript numbers slightly above the line in your paper. Place the number at the end of a sentence, clause, or phrase containing material you wish to document. Number the citations sequentially throughout your paper. (Do not, that is, begin a new set of numbers on each page on which you have notes.) Each number will correspond to an entry in your footnotes or endnotes. The following is an example:

Text

```
As Janetta Benton has noted, gargoyles are
usually located in "visually inaccessible
locations,"[1] peripheral to the medieval cathedral.
Benton also speculates that gargoyle sculptors can
be compared with medieval manuscript illuminators
in their artistic freedom and imaginativeness.[2]
```

Notes

¹ Janetta Rebold Benton, <u>The Medieval
Menagerie: Animals in the Art of the Middle Ages</u>
(New York: Abbeville, 1992) 57.
   ² Benton 58-59.

Guidelines for Footnotes and Endnotes

- Place endnotes at the end of the paper on a separate page headed "Notes." Double space to the first note entry and between entries. Single space within individual entries.
- Remember to key each superscript number in the text of your paper to a numbered note in your list of endnotes—or to the corresponding footnote at the bottom of the page on which the citation occurs.
- If you use footnotes, place them at the base of the page where the superscript number appears. Single space within individual footnotes but double space between different ones.
- Indent each note five spaces from the left margin. Follow the number with space. Bring subsequent lines of an entry to the margin, indenting only the first line.

Basic Format for Foonotes and Endnotes

For the first reference to a source:
Author's name in normal word order followed by a comma, the title of the source, the publication information in parentheses, and the page numbers. (See the Benton reference above.)

For the second and subsequent references to a source:
Author's last name and the page number(s) separated only by a space. When you use this short form for multiple citations to more than one work by the same author, include an abbreviated title in the entry.

Example

Benton, <u>Menagerie</u> 66.
Benton, <u>Terrors</u> 14.

Note the comma between author and short title in each entry.
   Here are sample citations for different kinds of sources you may need to note among the documented sources in your paper.

BOOKS

Book with One Author

¹ Janetta Rebold Benton, <u>The Medieval Menagerie: Animals in the Art of the Middle Ages</u> (New York: Abbeville, 1992) 57.

Book with Two or Three Authors

² Janetta Rebold Benton and Robert DiYanni, <u>Arts and Culture: An Introduction to the Humanities</u> (Englewood Cliffs NJ: Prentice-Hall, 1998) 256.

Book with More Than Three Authors

³ Sheryl Adams et al., <u>The Humanities for the New Millennium</u> (London: Faber, 2000) 24.

Book with an Anonymous Author

⁴ <u>The World Almanac and Book of Facts</u> (New York: NEA, 1983) 34–35.

Book with an Author and an Editor

⁵ <u>George Orwell, Orwell: The War Commentaries</u>, ed. W.J. West (New York: Pantheon, 1985) 210.

Book with an Editor

⁶ Robert DiYanni, ed. <u>Modern American Poets: Their Voices and Visions</u>, 2nd ed. (New York: 1993) 12.

Selection from an Anthology

⁷ Robert Hollander, "Dante's Authority," <u>Lectura Dantis: Inferno</u>, ed. Allen Mandelbaum, Antyony Oldcorn, and Charles Ross (Berkeley: U of California P, 1998) 33.

Multivolume Work

⁸ Joseph Blotner, <u>Faulkner: A Biography</u>, vol. 1 (New York: Random, 1987) 257.

PERIODICALS

Article in a Journal Paginated by Volume

⁹ Adelia Williams, "Jean Tardieu: The Painterly Poem," <u>Foreign Language Studies</u> 18 (1991): 119

Article in a Journal Paginated by Issue

¹⁰ Daniel Bender, "Diversity Revisited, or Composition's Alien History," <u>Rhetoric Review</u> 12.1 (1987): 115.

Review

¹¹ Edward Rothstein, "Blood and Thunder from the Young Verdi," rev. of <u>I Lombardi</u>, Metropolitan Opera House, New York. <u>New York Times</u> 4 Dec. 1993: C11.

Bibliography and Works Cited List

If you use a footnote or endnote format, you will list your sources at the very end of your paper (following your text and endnotes if you have those) on a separate sheet headed "Bibliography." Alphabetize your sources according to the last name of the author. Blend all sources in a single alphabetical listing, regardless of whether they are books or periodical articles from journals.

If you use the MLA in-text citation format for your notes, list your sources at the end of the paper and head the page "Works Cited." Alphabetize and blend as described above.

In both Bibliography and Works Cited lists, double space between the title and the first entry. Single space within each entry, but double space between different entries.

Begin each entry flush with the left margin, but indent all subsequent lines of the five character spaces. Sample entries for books, periodicals, and other sources, including electronic sources, follow.

BOOKS

Book with a Single Author

Benton, Janetta Rebold. <u>The Medieval Menagerie: Animals in the Art of the Middle Ages</u>. New York: Abbeville, 1992.

Book with Two or Three Authors

Benton, Janetta Rebold and Robert DiYanni. <u>Arts
    and Culture: An Introduction to the
    Humanities</u>. Englewood Cliffs NJ: Prentice-
    Hall, 1998.

Book with More Than Three Authors

Adams, Sheryl, et al. <u>The Humanities for the New
    Millennium</u>. London: Faber, 2000.

Book with an Anonymous Author

The World Almanac and Book of Facts. <u>New York:
    NEA, 1983</u>.

Book with an Author and an Editor

Orwell, George. <u>Orwell: The War Commentaries</u>. Ed.
    W.J. West. New York: Pantheon, 1985.

Book with an Editor

Foner, Eric and John A. Garraty, eds. <u>A Reader's
    Companion to American History</u>. Boston:
    Houghton, 1991.

Selection from an Anthology

Hollander, Robert. "Dante's Authority." <u>Lectura
    Dantis: Inferno</u>. Ed. Allen Mandelbaum,
    Anthony Oldcorn, and Charles Ross. Berkeley:
    U of California P, 1998. 25-35.

Multivolume Book

Malone, Dumas. <u>Jefferson and His Time</u>. 6 vols.
    Boston: Little, 1943-77.

Translation

Wilhelm, Richard. <u>Confucius and Confucianism</u>.
    Trans. George H. Danton and Annina Periam
    Danton. New York: Harcourt, 1931.

Revised Edition

Holloway, Mark. <u>Heavens on Earth: Utopian Communities in America, 1660-1880</u>. 2nd ed. New York: Dover, 1966.

Article in a Reference Book

"Cochise." <u>Encyclopedia of Indians of the Americas</u>. St. Clair Shores, MI: Scholarly, 1974.

PERIODICALS

Article in a Journal Paginated by Volume

Williams, Adelia. "Jean Tardieu: The Painterly Poem." <u>Foreign Language Studies</u> 18 (1991): 114-125.

Article in a Journal Paginated by Issue

Bender, Daniel. "Diversity Revisited, or Composition's Alien History." <u>Rhetoric Review</u> 12.1 (1987): 108-124.

Review

Rothstein, Edward. "Blood and Thunder from the Young Verdi." Rev. of <u>I Lombardi</u>. Metropolitan Opera House, New York. <u>New York Times</u> 4 Dec. 1993: C11.

MUSICAL COMPOSITION

Mozart, Wolfgang Amadeus. <u>Don Giovanni</u>.

WORK OF ART

Bernini, Gianlorenzo. <u>David</u>. Galleria Borghese, Rome.

FILM

The Age of Innocence. Dir. Martin Scorsese. Prod.
    Barbara DeFina. Perf. Daniel Day-Lewis,
    Michelle Pfeiffer, and Winona Ryder.
    Columbia, 1993.

RECORDING

Bartoli, Cecilia. The Impatient Lover: Italian
    Songs by Beethoven, Schubert, Haydn, and
    Mozart. Compact disc. London, 440 297-2, 1993.

MAP OR CHART

France. Map. Chicago: Rand, 1988.

ELECTRONIC SOURCES

Formats for citations of electronic sources, especially Internet sources, remain variable. Consult recent guides, such as the *MLA Handbook for Writers of Research Papers,* for updates on appropriate formats. You can use the following samples, however, to guide you in formatting electronic source citations.

CD, Tape, or Diskette Produced as a Single Publication

DeLorme Mapping. "Vestfirdhir [Iceland]." Global
    Explorer. CD-ROM. Freeport, ME: DeLorme,
    1993.

CD, Tape, or Diskette Updated Periodically

Lacayo, Richard. "This Land Is Whose Land?" Time
    23 Oct. 1995: 68-71. Academic ASAP. CD-ROM.
    Infotrac. Dec. 1995.

Online Sources

Shimabakuto, Jim, ed. "Internet in 10 Years--Essays."
    Electronic Journal on Virtual Culture 3.1
    (1995): 62 pars. Online. BITNET. 20 Oct. 1996.

APPENDIX

Writing Essay Examinations

Certainly the most common form of writing you will do, perhaps as frequently as you write essays, papers, and reports, is writing essay examinations, often in class. Writing strong essay examination answers is essential for success in many college humanities courses. Answering essay exam questions poses a challenge because you are often writing under the pressure of time. By following a few guidelines, you can improve your chances of doing well when you write essay exams.

- Be sure you understand the question. Make certain that you know what is expected of you. If you are unsure about a question, ask the instructor to clarify the test.
- Budget your time so you can answer all essay questions. Essay questions typically count heavily in an exam. Leaving out an entire question can seriously compromise your grade.
- Think before writing your essay answer. This may be difficult, because your tendency may be to begin writing immediately. But even in two or three minutes of silent thought, as you jot a few quick notes, your mind begins calling up evidence and ideas, and you can begin selecting key points and organizing them.
- Provide specific details and examples to support your general assertions. This is critical. Essay answers that omit specific references or concrete examples often reveal a lack of depth and persuasiveness. On the other hand, essay responses that contain only specific information may reveal a lack of understanding of connections and relationships among ideas and evidence. You need both facts and explanations, specific details in support of the ideas they explain and illustrate.

- Avoid padding your answer with irrelevant details. Instructors do not reward off-topic responses. Nor are they pleased by answers padded with unnecessary repetition. Include in your response only details—facts, statistics, examples—relevant to the question.
- Write legibly, and proofread your answers. Avoid the temptation to write so fast that your writing becomes unreadable. Check your paper for errors of spelling, punctuation, grammar, mechanics, and usage. Error-ridden answers can be distracting to readers. They also reveal a lack of control on the part of the writer.

These guidelines must be seen in relation to how much time you have to write each essay question. If you are unsure of how much time is allotted for essay questions, ask your instructor. To understand the nature of the task prompted by the question, study its wording carefully.

PREPARING FOR AN EXAM

You begin preparing for an exam not long before you study specifically for it a day or a week before. Your real exam preparation occurs in the classwork and homework you do throughout the course. Effective exam preparation includes careful note taking during class and during assigned reading. In reviewing your notes for an essay exam, be alert for patterns and connections among facts, examples, concepts, and theories as explained in lectures and readings. Essay exams will often require you to synthesize information and to explain relationships among important events and critical ideas. They may also ask you to evaluate ideas and events.

Review and study the course material carefully. You may wish to form a study group with a few other students. Study groups allow you to compare notes with those of others to assess your understanding of concepts and relationships among ideas. Study groups also give you a chance to create sample questions and to test each other. This kind of practice not only helps prepare you for the types of questions that may appear on the exam, but it also may help to reduce your anxiety in taking the actual examination.

The most important kind of preparation you can do for any type of essay examination is to find ways to relate and connect the information, examples, and concepts you have learned. You need to find ways to fit the various parts and pieces together. For example, in learning about the id in a psychology class, be sure you understand its relationship to the ego and superego. In learning about the social causes of the Russian Revolution, consider the importance of economic and political contexts as well. In studying the Russian Revolution in a course on modern revolutions, relate its various causes to the causes of other early twentieth-century revolutions such as the Mexican Revolution. Make connections and identify relationships as much as you can during every phase of preparing for an exam.

EXERCISE

Look back over notes for one of your current courses. In the left margin use a different color ink to make connections with facts, information, and concepts on different pages by cross-referencing them.

REVIEWING THE QUESTIONS

Read the questions carefully—two or three times, if possible. Avoid jumping immediately to a conclusion about what the instructor is asking. Look carefully at the wording of each question. Does it ask you to "discuss," "define," "compare," "evaluate"? Perhaps it asks you to "define and analyze," "compare and contrast," "identify and explain." Be sure that you understand precisely what the question requires you to do. If you are unsure, ask.

Many college exam questions ask for analysis and interpretation. For such questions you are expected not merely to give back information, but to use information to make a general analytical or interpretive point—to explain, that is, the significance of information. For example, you can expect not merely to summarize the plot of a novel but to analyze its structural relationships; that is, how its parts or sections develop and fit together.

Here are some examples of common terms used in essay exams and the kinds of questions in which they often appear.

Identify means "to name, indicate, or specify." Some essay exams include "identify' as part of a question that asks you to "identify and explain" or "identify and discuss."

Example

Identify and explain the significance of the following quotation: "If a man does not keep pace with his companions, perhaps it is because he hears the sound of a different drummer. Let him step to the music which he hears, however measured or far away."

Explain means "to give reasons for, to relate causes and effects, to identify a process." Explanations can be simple or complex, brief or elaborate. The time limit for an essay response requiring explanation will determine how fully developed your explanation can be.

Example

Explain why Georg Friedrich Handel began writing oratorios and stopped writing operas. Explain also the difference between an opera and an oratorio.

Discuss means "to write about." This generalized instruction seems more general than other exam instructions. Often, however, "discuss" is used to mean "identify and explain."

Example

Discuss the structure and function of sonata form.

For this topic, you would be expected to identify the elements of sonata form and to explain how composers used sonata form in their symphonies, sonatas, and concertos.

Define means "to provide a definition, to point out characteristic features, to identify limits, or to put something into a category or class." Definitions can be brief or extended. An essay question that asks you to define a term or a concept may also require you to explain, exemplify, characterize, or further discuss various aspects or element of your definition.

Example

Define the concept of affirmative action. Discuss the historical roots of the concept, and consider the social and cultural issues and forces that have led to its emergence as a contemporary problem.

Compare means "to consider similarities and differences between two things." More precisely, the word *compare* invites consideration of similarities and the word *contrast,* differences. But often *compare* is used to mean "identify and explain similarities and differences between X and Y."

Example

Compare Michelangelo's sculpture of David with Bernini's.

Analyze means "to break into parts." You identify the individual components of a painting, for example, the better to understand each element and the better to understand the relationship of the parts or elements to the work as a whole.

Example

Analyze Velazquez's *Las Meninas.* Be sure to consider the elements of space and light the painter has created in this work, as well as his positioning of figures.

Evaluate means "to assess or make a judgment about." You may be asked to evaluate the claims made by competing theories, such as creationism and evolution as explanations of the origins of human life. You may be asked to evaluate the persuasiveness of an idea or argument. Sometimes evaluation may involve comparison and contrast.

Example

Evaluate the performance of Mel Gibson in the role of Hamlet.

(Here, for example, you might compare Gibson's performance in this role with that of other actors such as Lawrence Olivier or Kenneth Branagh—if you saw their film versions of *Hamlet.* Or you might compare Gibson's performance in the role of Hamlet with his performance of a major role in another of his films.)

WRITING YOUR ANSWER

Once you have read and understood the question, take a few minutes to think before you begin writing your answer. Consider what you want to say and how you might use your knowledge to support an idea you have. Collect your thoughts, recall information, and begin to sort and relate facts and ideas.

Taking account of the time allotted for the question, plan on developing an answer accordingly. For a sixty-minute exam with three essay questions, unless otherwise stipulated, allot twenty minutes to each.

Begin with some preliminary writing, jotting a few rough notes. You can arrange your notes, after you think of a number of details, examples, and ideas, simply by numbering them before you write your essay response. The act of putting pen to paper will help you think of what to write—as long as you are well prepared. You will discover additional connections as you write, but even before beginning, you should have a general idea of how to start and conclude, with a few points to cover in between. Making a rough preliminary outline of where you are heading in your answer and how to get there will decrease the chances that you will forget something important.

It is very important to make your thesis, the central point of your essay, clear from the start. Because essay exam questions have strict time constraints, make sure to get your major point across clearly and quickly.

As you write, be sure to respond directly to the question. Avoid vagueness and bland generalizations that say very little. Also avoid trying to throw everything you can think of into your answer, in the hopes that a scattershot approach will score at least a partial hit. Instead, tackle the question head on.

Example

Discuss the political factors that led up to the French Revolution.

This question requires an answer that addresses political factors only—not military, economic, or social ones (unless, of course, you can show how those other kinds of factors directly relate to the political issues the question asks about).

On the other hand, you should not answer a broad question too narrowly. Respond to a question that asks for a discussion of the central tenets of European Romanticism by including references to more than a single country and a single artistic area. Don't limit yourself, for example, to discussing only Romantic music in Austria or Romantic poetry in England.

ADDITIONAL ADVICE

Because you will have time for only a single draft in writing essay exams, it is important to stay focused on the question, to include the most important ideas and kinds of evidence, and to conclude your answer by reiterating a key point or explaining an important or interesting ramification of it.

Be sure to reserve some time to review your answer. Try to allow for even a few minutes for reviewing your writing. In your review you may discover that you overlooked a telling detail, a significant issue, or a critical fact. Or you may realize that you omitted a word or phrase whose omission makes your sentence unintelligible. By leaving out a word like *not,* you may actually suggest the opposite of what you intend.

When you run short of time in an essay exam, map out the direction your essay would take if you had the time to complete it. Provide an outline that shows your instructor what you intended to discuss. Depending on how specific you can make the outline and on how accurate and thorough your answer has been up to that point, you are more likely to be given the benefit of the doubt and score higher than if you were simply to stop midway through.

The following guidelines summarize key strategies for writing essay examinations.

- Prepare yourself for the exam well in advance.
- Read and analyze the question carefully.
- Think before writing.
- Make some notes and a scratch outline to start.
- Identify your central idea or thesis early on.
- Respond directly to the demands of the question.
- Review and check your answer.

EXERCISE

Analyze the following questions:

1. Explain Darwin's theory of evolution by natural selection. In your answer include specific examples of species that Darwin and other scientists observed to lead them to their evolutionist conclusions.

2. Analyze the logic of organization of Dante's Hell (Inferno). Consider the principle of symbolic retribution, and supply examples to illustrate your remarks.

3. Explain the change in Hamlet's behavior that emerges from the beginning to the end of the play. Explain what prompts Hamlet's change of mind/attitude/behavior, and consider its significance.

4. Discuss the way nature is depicted and characterized in two of the following:

> **a.** a Chinese landscape painter
>
> **b.** Japanese gardens
>
> **c.** a European or American painter of the nineteenth century
>
> **d.** a European or American poet of the nineteenth or twentieth century

5. Compare and contrast the Renaissance painting styles prevalent in Holland and Italy.

6. Define the term *Impressionism.* Identify its most notable practitioners in two different fields of the arts. Explain how their work fits the definition of Impressionism you provide.

ACKNOWLEDGMENTS

TEXT

Page 5: "The Starry Night" from ALL MY PRETTY ONES by Anne Sexton. Copyright © 1962 by Anne Sexton, © renewed 1990 by Linda G. Sexton. Reprinted by permission of Houghton Mifflin Company. All rights reserved.

Page 13: "The Erl King" by Franz Peter Schubert from THE PENGUIN BOOK OF LIEDER (pp. 34–35, 32 lines) edited and translated by S. S. Prawer (Penguin Books, 1964). Copyright © S. S. Prawer, 1964. Reproduced by permission of Penguin Books, Ltd.

Page 92: "Stopping by Woods on a Snowy Evening" by Robert Frost. From THE POETRY OF ROBERT FROST edited by Edward Connery Lathem. Copyright © 1923, © 1969 Henry Holt & Company, copyright © 1951 by Robert Frost. Reprinted by permission of Henry Holt & Company, L.L.C.

Page 93: "My People" by Langston Hughes. From COLLECTED POEMS by Langston Hughes. Copyright © 1994 by the Estate of Langston Hughes. Reprinted by permission of Alfred A. Knopf, Inc.

Pages 95–97: "Andre's Mother." Copyright © 1995 by Terrence McNally. Reprinted by permission of the William Morris Agency on behalf of the author.

PHOTOS

Page 4: The Museum of Modern Art, New York, acquired through the Lillie P. Bliss Bequest. **Pages 7 and 72 (right):** Corbis/Gianni Dagli Orti. **Page 43:** Collection of The New York Historical Society. **Page 44:** Art Resource, N.Y./Eric Lessing. **Page 48:** National Gallery of Art, Washington, D.C., Rosenwald Collection. **Page 49:** Corbis/Brustein Collection. **Page 67:** (*top*) Detroit Institute of Arts, Thomas Cole; (*bottom*) © The Cleveland Museum of Art, Mr. and Mrs. William H. Marlatt Fund. **Page 70:** (*top*) Magnum Photos, Inc.; (*bottom*) © Estate of Dmitri Baltermants, courtesy G. Ray Hawkins Gallery, Santa Monica. **Page 72 (left):** Corbis/Roger Antrobus. **Page 129:** Yale University Art Gallery. Whitney Collections of Sporting Art, given in memory of Harry Payne Whitney, B.A. 1894, and Payne Whitney, B.A. 1898, by Francis P. Garvan, M.A. 1897, M.A. (Hon.) 1922.

INDEX

Page references in italics refer to illustrations.